Reading Excellence: Word Attack & Rate Development Strategies

Reading Strategies
~ Applied to ~
# Science Passages

Anita L. Archer, Ph.D.
Mary M. Gleason, Ph.D.
Vicky Vachon, Ph.D.

Assisted by
Beth Cooper
Ken Shindledecker
Pat Pielaet
Melody McIntosh

SOPRIS WEST EDUCATIONAL SERVICES
A CAMBIUM LEARNING COMPANY

BOSTON, MA • NEW YORK, NY • LONGMONT, CO

Cover photograph of Rachel Carson courtesy of Lear Carson Collection,
Connecticut College: Photo by Brooks Studio
Cover photograph of leopard © DigitalVision/PictureQuest
Cover photograph of tornado © Comstock Images
Cover photograph of earth/satellite/sun © Scott Tysick/Masterfile

ISBN 1-59318-286-4
ISBN 1-59318-287-2 (Student Book Set)

Edited by Sandra L. Knauke
Text layout and design by Edward Horcharik
Cover design by Sherri Rowe
Illustrations by Kathy Bone

09 08 07 06 05   5 4 3 2 1

Printed in the United States of America
Published and Distributed by

SOPRIS
WEST
EDUCATIONAL SERVICES

4093 Specialty Place • Longmont, Colorado 80504
(303) 651-2829 • www.sopriswest.com

136SCISTU/8-04/BAN/50M/086

CONTENTS

(ACTIVITY A) *Vowel Combinations*

ay	ai	au	
(say)	(rain)	(sauce)	

er	ir	ur	ar
(her)	(bird)	(turn)	(farm)

(ACTIVITY B) *Vowel Conversions*

a   i   o

(ACTIVITY C) *Word Parts at the Beginning and End of Words*

(dis)cover	dis	(ad)vertise	ad
(mis)taken	mis	(in)sert	in
(ab)domen	ab	(im)mediate	im

(ACTIVITY D) *Strategy Instruction*

1. abstract	insist	impact
2. distraught	misfit	admit

(ACTIVITY E) *Strategy Practice*

1. birthday	misplay	discard
2. maintain	disband	indistinct
3. modern	addict	imprint
4. absurd	insert	railway

(ACTIVITY F) *Sentence Reading*

1. John wanted to disband his rock group after they played at the birthday party.
2. The author will insist on reading the abstract from his new book.
3. She was very distraught when her mother tried to discard her old clothes.
4. The teacher will maintain that her words were right.
5. They will admit that they left imprints of their hands on the glass.
6. As a misfit, the puppy spent most of its time by itself.
7. Her shouts were so absurd that she was asked to leave.
8. Their modern ways of doing things had a strong impact on the group.
9. He tried his best to help the team, but he would often misplay the baseball.
10. The animal's tracks in the mud were indistinct.

ACTIVITY A *Vowel Combinations*

a—e	o—e	i—e	e—e	u—e
(make)	(hope)	(side)	(Pete)	(use)

1.	er	ir	au	ai	a—e
2.	ar	u—e	ay	i—e	au
3.	e—e	ir	ai	o—e	u—e
4.	ur	ay	a—e	au	i—e

ACTIVITY B *Vowel Conversions*

a	i	o	u

ACTIVITY C *Word Parts at the Beginning and End of Words*

compare	com	prevent	pre
belong	be	protect	pro
return	re	depart	de

1.	pro	be	pre	ad	dis	mis
2.	com	in	im	re	ab	de

(ACTIVITY D) *Strategy Instruction*

1.	beside	readjust	prepay
2.	combine	provide	defraud

(ACTIVITY E) *Strategy Practice*

1.	backbone	reprint	costume
2.	mistake	promote	prescribe
3.	obsolete	propose	sunstroke
4.	decode	holiday	subscribe

(ACTIVITY F) *Sentence Reading*

1. She wanted to subscribe to her favorite magazine.
2. The costume was worn to promote the holiday.
3. Sunstroke can happen if you stay outside in the sun too long.
4. He needed to readjust how he took notes once the splint was put on his arm.
5. It is easy to decode long words such as **provide** and **mistake**.
6. I propose we take a trip on the railway, but we will have to prepay our tickets.
7. When people are brave, they are said to have a lot of backbone.
8. Doctors often prescribe some type of pill when people are not feeling well.
9. The con man tried to defraud the old people of their life savings.
10. The magazine story was obsolete, so we couldn't order a reprint.

ACTIVITY A *Vowel Combinations*

oi	oy	or
(void)	(boy)	(torn)
ee	oa	ou
(deep)	(foam)	(loud)

1. er   a—e   oi   oy   ee

2. u—e   ou   au   or   oa

3. e—e   ir   ai   i—e   ar

4. o—e   ur   ay   au   ou

ACTIVITY B *Vowel Conversions*

a   i   o   u   e

ACTIVITY C *Word Parts at the Beginning and End of Words*

continue	con	above	a
permit	per	example	ex
uncover	un	entail	en

1. per   con   dis   a   pre   de

2. com   pro   en   ab   im   mis

3. ex   con   un   com   a   pre

(ACTIVITY D) *Strategy Practice*

1. perturb	uncurl	confess
2. afraid	expert	engrave

(ACTIVITY E) *Independent Strategy Practice*

1. misinform	disagree	spellbound
2. sweepstake	reproduce	protect
3. turmoil	bemoan	discontent
4. imperfect	boycott	reconstruct

(ACTIVITY F) *Sentence Reading*

1. Please do not misinform people about the boycott on those items.
2. Don't be afraid to disagree with certain ideas.
3. The man tried to reproduce the painting, but the result was imperfect.
4. He did confess that the turmoil began on the baseball field.
5. I won't bemoan the fact that I did not win the sweepstakes money.
6. It will perturb him to find out that the expert could not protect him.
7. The dancers were so good that they left the people spellbound.
8. Did he engrave the wedding ring for you?
9. They tried to reconstruct the building, but those who paid them were discontent.
10. We always disagree on how much to invest in the stock market.

ACTIVITY A *Vowel Combinations*

ow

(low)   (down)

1.	ou	ow	i—e	oy	ur
2.	oa	a—e	ow	ai	ir
3.	oi	ow	ee	ow	ar
4.	au	or	oy	u—e	ow

ACTIVITY B *Vowel Conversions*

u   e   i   a   o

ACTIVITY C *Word Parts at the Beginning and End of Words*

birds	s	frantic	ic
running	ing	regulate	ate
landed	ed	selfish	ish
		artist	ist
kindness	ness	realism	ism
useless	less	biggest	est
final	al	tailor	or
careful	ful	farmer	er

1.	ab	com	con	dis	pre	re
2.	im	ex	un	per	pro	a
3.	est	ic	ful	or	al	er
4.	ish	ism	less	ate	ness	ist

(ACTIVITY D) *Strategy Practice*

1. regardless	softness	unfortunate
2. programmer	slowest	historical
3. organism	inventor	personal

(ACTIVITY E) *Independent Strategy Practice*

1. abnormal	respectful	proposal
2. exaggerate	exhaust	untruthful
3. careless	unfaithful	astonish
4. alarmist	energetic	exclude

(ACTIVITY F) *Sentence Reading*

1. It is so unfortunate that the programmer quit in the middle of the project.
2. The inventor exaggerated his claims for a modern submarine.
3. Would you be astonished to know that she was excluded from the group?
4. Regardless of how untruthful he was about the money, he is not a careless man.
5. It is not abnormal for many types of organisms to exist in the same area.
6. His proposal was too astonishing to be used, regardless of his background.
7. The historical display exaggerated the inventor's role.
8. She was an alarmist but was not careless with her words or unfaithful to her beliefs.
9. He decided to take the slowest way home for the holidays.
10. She was so energetic that her friends became exhausted whenever they were with her.

ACTIVITY A *Vowel Combinations*

oo

(moon)   (book)

1. ow	oa	oi	oo	oy
2. ee	ou	er	ir	au
3. ay	oo	a—e	ur	oo
4. ar	ai	ow	oo	au

ACTIVITY B *Vowel Conversions*

e   i   a   u   o

ACTIVITY C *Word Parts at the Beginning and End of Words*

action	tion	military	ary
mission	sion	oddity	ity
million	ion	dormant	ant
attentive	tive	disturbance	ance
expensive	sive	consistent	ent
industry	y	essence	ence
safely	ly	argument	ment

1. al	con	a	com	er
2. tion	or	ly	sive	ance
3. tive	ary	ence	ent	ant
4. ity	ment	y	ion	est
5. ful	ity	sion	ance	ant

(ACTIVITY D) *Strategy Practice*

1. advertisement	delightful	disinfectant
2. intentionally	property	expressionless
3. personality	admittance	incoherence

(ACTIVITY E) *Independent Strategy Practice*

1. perfectionist	independently	dictionary
2. contaminate	precautionary	deductive
3. inconsistently	excitement	repulsive
4. opinion	hoodwink	imperfect

(ACTIVITY F) *Sentence Reading*

1. The members took a precautionary approach when considering her application for admittance to the club.

2. As a perfectionist, she had a strong reaction to the imperfect dictionary.

3. When told that his actions might contaminate the experiment, his face was expressionless.

4. The advertisement for disinfectant was delightful but intentionally inaccurate.

5. He came to his opinion through deductive problem-solving.

6. John came to his own conclusions independently.

7. Unfortunately, the only excitement came at the end of the performance.

8. She did not try to hoodwink him regarding the value of the property.

9. The drawing was imperfect but was not repulsive.

10. The homework assignments were lengthy and were inconsistently completed by most students.

(ACTIVITY A) *Vowel Combinations*

ea

(meat)   (thread)

1.	oo	ea	ow	ee	er	ai
2.	au	ay	e—e	oy	ea	ur
3.	oa	i—e	ir	ea	ar	oi
4.	ow	ur	ea	oo	oi	au

(ACTIVITY B) *Vowel Conversions Review*

u   i   a   e   o

(ACTIVITY C) *Word Parts at the Beginning and End of Words*

nervous   ous   courage   age
precious   cious   picture   ture
cautious   tious   disposable   able
special   cial   reversible   ible
partial   tial   cradle   le

1.	per	a	con	com	ex
2.	ous	able	ment	le	ent
3.	al	age	ture	cious	tial
4.	ion	ible	y	ance	or
5.	ity	cial	ence	ant	tious

(ACTIVITY D) *Strategy Practice*

1. official	substantial	delicious
2. pretentious	impressionable	incombustible
3. conjecture	inconspicuous	disadvantage

(ACTIVITY E) *Independent Strategy Practice*

1. administrative	performance	threadbare
2. circumstantial	investigation	professionalism
3. precipitation	environmentally	communication
4. unconventional	consolidate	misconception

(ACTIVITY F) *Sentence Reading*

1. The unprofessional official took a substantial bribe before beginning the investigation.

2. His administrative performance showed tremendous professionalism.

3. Circumstantial evidence was not enough to convict the defendant.

4. Precipitation in the form of sleet leaves motorists at a distinct disadvantage.

5. There was substantial truth in his communication, but it still led to serious misconceptions.

6. If you wish to consolidate services, you will need to ensure environmentally safe conditions for all employees.

7. The unconventional approach to the investigation led to much conjecture.

8. Because she was so impressionable, she was at a disadvantage.

9. Even though her advisor gave good advice, she refused to consolidate her investments.

10. Although his actions were usually pretentious, his presence at the lecture was totally inconspicuous.

ACTIVITY A *Vocabulary*

List 1: Tell

1. scientists   *n.* ▶ (people with expert knowledge of science)
2. universe   *n.* ▶ (all things that exist, including our solar system and beyond)
3. organisms   *n.* ▶ (all living things, including all plants and animals)
4. ecosystem   *n.* ▶ (a living community of organisms and their physical environment)
5. climate   *n.* ▶ (the pattern of weather conditions in an area or region)
6. bacteria   *n.* ▶ (very tiny single-celled organisms)
7. fungus   *n.* ▶ (a plant-like organism without leaves, flowers, or green coloring)
8. fungi   *n.* ▶ (more than one fungus; the plural of fungus)
9. protists   *n.* ▶ (usually single-celled organisms that have both plant and animal characteristics)

List 2: Strategy Practice

1. interactions   *n.* ▶ (actions or influences on each other)
2. population   *n.* ▶ (the number of organisms living in an area)
3. function   *v.* ▶ (to act or operate normally; to perform)
4. tropical   *adj.* ▶ (very humid and hot or having to do with the tropics)
5. available   *adj.* ▶ (ready to be used)
6. requirements   *n.* ▶ (things that are needed or depended upon)
7. nutrients   *n.* ▶ (matter needed by plants and animals so they can live)
8. predator   *n.* ▶ (an animal that hunts or kills another for food)
9. eventually   *adv.* ▶ (finally)
10. extinction   *n.* ▶ (the end of or the dying out of a type of plant or animal)

TALLY [　　　]   VOCABULARY **5**

Points

List 3: Word Relatives

	Verb	Noun	Adjective
Family 1	energize (to give energy)	energy energizer	energetic
Family 2	consume (to eat)	consumer consumption	consumable
Family 3	transform (to change)	transformation transformer	
Family 4	capture (to catch or attract)	captive captor	
Family 5	compose (to make or create)	composition composer	composite

ACTIVITY B *Spelling Dictation*

1.	4.
2.	5.
3.	6.

(ACTIVITY C) *Passage Reading and Comprehension*

Note: For this activity, you will need Reproducible A found in the *Teacher's Guide*.

Ecosystems

A

14   The universe is a very complex system, in which all things interact with each
other. Within this complex system are many different systems called

24   **ecosystems**. An ecosystem is composed of living things interacting with other

35   living things and with nonliving things such as weather, soil, and water. Earth's

48   ecosystems may be as large as an ocean or as small as a drop of water. Forests,

65   rivers, and meadows are examples of ecosystems. (#1)

72   **Energy and Matter in Ecosystems**

77   All organisms within an ecosystem require a steady supply of energy and

89   matter for their life processes. These life processes include growing, developing,

100   reproducing, and responding to their surroundings. (#2)

106   All energy and matter that organisms require must be available within their

118   ecosystem. Most energy comes from the sun. Plants and tiny organisms (protists

130   and bacteria) capture the sun's energy and transform it into food energy (matter)

143   for themselves and other organisms. These other organisms cannot make their

154   own food, so they consume the tiny organisms and plants (or parts of plants). (#3)

168   Eventually, the organisms die. Their dead bodies become food for bacteria

179   and fungi. The bacteria and fungi return nutrients to the soil, where the plants

193   use them, and the cycling of energy and matter begins again. (#4)

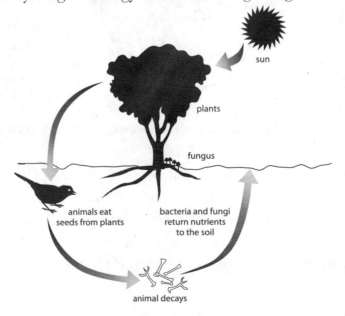

The Energy Cycle

Interactions Within Ecosystems

B	204	
	207	
	217	
	227	
	238	
	250	
	263	
	277	
	287	
	305	
	317	
	332	

B 204 | **Interactions Within Ecosystems**

207 | Larger organisms not only consume tiny organisms and plants, larger
217 | organisms also interact with other organisms within their ecosystem. Sometimes,
227 | these interactions are friendly and benefit both organisms. For example, bees
238 | benefit when they gather pollen and nectar from flowers. These substances are
250 | food for the bees. Flowers benefit because the bees' gathering activities help to
263 | move the pollen from one flower to another so the flowers can make seeds. (#5)

277 | Another interaction that benefits two organisms is the special relationship
287 | that exists when a type of fungus finds a home in and on the roots of trees. This
305 | fungus absorbs water and minerals from the surrounding soil and shares these
317 | with the tree. The tree uses these raw materials to make a sugary food, which
332 | the fungus feeds on. Large forests depend on this special relationship. (#6)

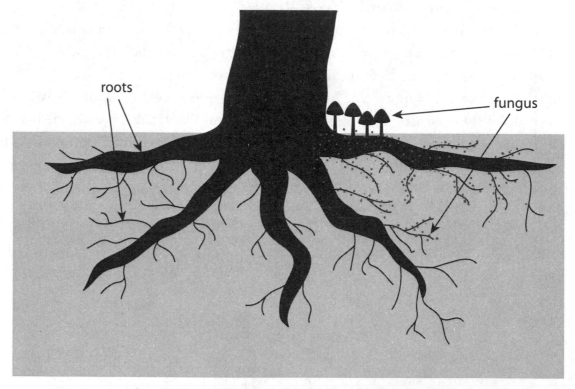

Special Relationship Between Fungus and Tree Roots

343 | Other interactions appear not to be so friendly. One example is the predator-
356 | prey relationship between the snake and the mouse. It seems as if only the
370 | snake benefits from eating the mouse, but actually, the population of mice in the
384 | ecosystem is helped. Snakes (the predators) keep the numbers of mice in
396 | balance with the supply of mouse food available. (#7)

Changes in Ecosystems

C	404
	407
	419
	430
	441
	452

Every species has its own special set of requirements for living. Because every ecosystem has its own climate and mineral makeup, each ecosystem supports a unique variety of species. The tropical rainforest ecosystem differs from the cooler, temperate rainforest. The desert ecosystem looks barren, but many special creatures that can survive only in those conditions live there. (#8)

| 464 |
| 477 |
| 490 |
| 502 |

An ecosystem will be greatly changed when parts of it are altered or removed. An entire ecosystem may cease to function properly if a group of living things are removed, new organisms are introduced, or dramatic long-term changes in climate occur. It may even cease to function altogether. (#9)

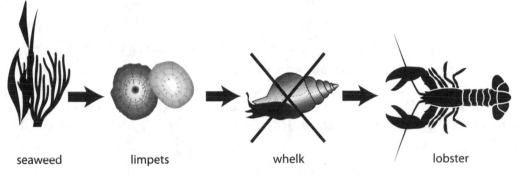

seaweed   limpets   whelk   lobster

A Threatened Ecosystem

| 513 |
| 526 |
| 538 |
| 549 |
| 561 |
| 576 |

Large changes in the earth's climate have led to mass extinctions of animals. For example, the extinction of dinosaurs has been linked to global climate changes. With drastic climate change, organisms that normally capture the sun's energy and pump it into the ecosystem may not survive. When organisms become extinct, the rest of the organisms in the ecosystem may not be able to survive in the same way as before. (#10)

| 583 |
| 595 |
| 607 |
| 620 |
| 631 |
| 643 |

For many years, scientists have been observing and measuring changes in the Earth's climate and in various ecosystems. Some of these changes have been natural and others were caused by human activities. In spite of their efforts, scientists still cannot predict the specific effects of changes to ecosystems; however, they are certain that any changes will affect the larger system. (#11)

(ACTIVITY D) *Fluency Building*

Cold Timing		Practice 1	

Practice 2		Hot Timing	

(ACTIVITY E) *Comprehension Questions—Multiple Choice*

Comprehension Strategy—Multiple Choice

Step 1: Read the item.

Step 2: Read all of the choices.

Step 3: Think about why each choice might be correct or incorrect. Check the article as needed.

Step 4: From the possible correct choices, select the best answer.

1. (Vocabulary) **The central vocabulary term in this article is "ecosystem." Which of the following is <u>NOT</u> true of an "ecosystem?"**

    a. A forest is an example of an ecosystem.

    b. Ecosystems are all very large.

    c. Organisms in an ecosystem need energy and matter to survive.

    d. A drastic change in climate can threaten the organisms in an ecosystem.

2. (Cause and effect) **If a small organism, such as a crab, does not have a steady supply of energy and matter in its ecosystem, what is most likely to occur?**

    a. The organism would migrate to a new ecosystem.

    b. The organism may need to become a predator in order to have a new food supply.

    c. The organism will not survive.

    d. The organism will need to interact with another organism in the ecosystem.

3. (Cause and effect) **Flowers benefit from interacting with bees in an ecosystem because:**

    a. the bees produce honey from the flower's nectar.

    b. the bees move nectar from one flower to another.

    c. the bees move pollen from one flower to another.

    d. the flowers use the nectar from other plants to produce seeds.

4. (Main idea) **Which sentence gives the best summary of the article?**

    a. Interactions between organisms in an ecosystem always benefit both organisms.

    b. Ecosystems can be as large as a forest or as small as a drop of water.

    c. In an ecosystem, organisms interact with other organisms and must have a supply of energy and matter.

    d. A climate change can lead to extinction of a species.

MULTIPLE CHOICE COMPREHENSION

4

(**ACTIVITY F**) *Vocabulary Activities*

Yes/No/Why

1. Are all **organisms predators**?

_____

_____

_____

_____

2. Do all living things have **nutrient requirements**?

_____

_____

_____

_____

3. Can **ecosystems** have **tropical climates**?

_____

_____

_____

_____

Completion Activity

1. capture: to catch or attract
You might capture your friends' attention by

_____

_____

_____

_____

2. consume: to eat
When you arrive home from school, you like to consume

_____

_____

_____

_____

3. eventually: finally
Homework tasks that you dislike but eventually finish include

_____

_____

_____

_____

4. extinction: the end of or the dying out of a type of plant or animal
Many types of organisms are threatened with extinction as a result of

_____

_____

_____

_____

VOCABULARY 7

(ACTIVITY G) *Expository Writing—Multi-Paragraph Answer*

Writing Strategy—Multi-Paragraph Answer

Step 1: **LIST** (List the details that are important enough to include in your answer.)
{ Step 2: **CROSS OUT** (Reread the details. Cross out any that don't go with the topic.)
Step 3: **CONNECT** (Connect any details that could go into one sentence.)
Step 4: **NUMBER** (Number the details in a logical order.)
Step 5: **WRITE** (Write the paragraph.)
Step 6: **EDIT** (Revise and proofread your answer.)

Prompt: What are three important things about ecosystems?

Plan: Complete the Planning Box with your teacher.

Example Multi-Paragraph Plan

Planning Box
(topic a) *organisms need energy and matter*
(detail) – *necessary for all life processes*
(detail) – *for growing, developing, reproducing, and responding to environment*
(detail) – *plants capture energy from sun and make into food for themselves and other organisms*
(detail) – *ecosystems can be very large or very small*
(topic b) *organisms interact with other organisms and with nonliving things*
(detail) – *friendly interactions benefit both organisms*
(detail) – *some interactions less friendly*
(topic c) *changes in ecosystem can affect how ecosystem functions*
(detail) – *may not function properly*
(detail) – *may cease to function at all*
(detail) – *extinction of organisms possible, especially if change in climate*

Write: Examine paragraphs a, b, and c with your teacher.

Example Multi-Paragraph Answer

(paragraph a)

   One important thing about ecosystems is that all organisms need energy and matter. Energy and matter are necessary for all life processes including growing, developing, reproducing, and responding to the environment. Plants capture energy from the sun and make it into food for themselves and other organisms.

(paragraph b)

   In addition, all organisms within an ecosystem interact with other organisms and with nonliving things. In many cases, the interactions between the organisms are friendly and both benefit. For example, both the bee and the flower profit from their interactions. However, some interactions, such as those between prey and predator, are less friendly.

(paragraph c)

   Another important idea about ecosystems is that changes in the ecosystem can affect how the ecosystem functions. If a major change occurs, the ecosystem may not function at all or at least not properly. If there is a major change in the climate, this can lead to extinction of organisms within an ecosystem.

Evaluate: Evaluate the paragraphs using this rubric.

Rubric— Multi-Paragraph Answer	Student or Partner Rating	Teacher Rating
1. Did the author state the topic in the first sentence?	a. Yes Fix up b. Yes Fix up c. Yes Fix up	a. Yes No b. Yes No c. Yes No
2. Did the author include details that go with the topic?	a. Yes Fix up b. Yes Fix up c. Yes Fix up	a. Yes No b. Yes No c. Yes No
3. Did the author combine details in some of the sentences?	a. Yes Fix up b. Yes Fix up c. Yes Fix up	a. Yes No b. Yes No c. Yes No
4. Is the answer easy to understand?	Yes Fix up	Yes No
5. Did the author correctly spell words, particularly the words found in the article?	Yes Fix up	Yes No
6. Did the author use correct capitalization, capitalizing the first word in the sentence and proper names of people, places, and things?	Yes Fix up	Yes No
7. Did the author use correct punctuation, including a period at the end of each sentence?	Yes Fix up	Yes No

WRITING 13 *Points*

(ACTIVITY H) *Comprehension—Single-Paragraph Answer*

Writing Strategy—Single-Paragraph Answer

Step 1: Read the item.
Step 2: Turn the question into part of the answer and write it down.
Step 3: Think of the answer or locate the answer in the article.
Step 4: Complete your answer.

Prompt:

What Is—Humans are part of an ecosystem and their activities may change the ecosystem in a number of ways.

What If—What might happen to the ecosystem if a new, large shopping mall was built on the forested outskirts of a city where there were few houses and roads?

Write and Discuss: Write a paragraph. Then share your ideas. Use the Discussion Guidelines.

Example Single-Paragraph Answer

If a large shopping mall was built on the forested outskirts of a city, a number of things might happen to the ecosystem. First, because the plants will be destroyed, they will be unable to transform energy from the sun into food needed by other organisms. Therefore, other organisms will not have the energy and matter that they require for life. These organisms will eventually die unless they are able to migrate to surrounding wooded areas. I would not expect a climate change from one mall. However, continued widespread construction might even begin to affect the climate.

Discussion Guidelines

Speaker		Listener	
Looks like:	**Sounds like:**	**Looks like:**	**Sounds like:**
• Facing peers • Making eye contact • Participating	• Using pleasant, easy-to-hear voice • Sharing opinions, supporting facts and reasons from the article and from your experience • Staying on the topic	• Facing speaker • Making eye contact • Participating	• Waiting quietly to speak • Giving positive, supportive comments • Disagreeing respectfully

(ACTIVITY A) *Vocabulary*

List 1: Tell

1.	**photosynthesis**	*n.* ▶	(the process by which green plants use the sun's energy to make food)
2.	**synthesis**	*n.* ▶	(putting things together)
3.	**chlorophyll**	*n.* ▶	(the green substance found in most plants)
4.	**chloroplasts**	*n.* ▶	(parts of the leaf in which photosynthesis takes place)
5.	**glucose**	*n.* ▶	(a simple sugar)
6.	**molecule**	*n.* ▶	(a very small amount, formed by combining atoms)
7.	**carbon dioxide**	*n.* ▶	(a colorless, odorless gas occurring naturally)
8.	**cellular**	*adj.* ▶	(related to cells)
9.	**microbes**	*n.* ▶	(very tiny living organisms)
10.	**uniquely**	*adv.* ▶	(unusually)
11.	**integral**	*adj.* ▶	(necessary for something to be whole)
12.	**resources**	*n.* ▶	(things that are ready to use to meet needs)

List 2: Strategy Practice

1.	**respiration**	*n.* ▶	(the action of breathing)
2.	**essential**	*adj.* ▶	(absolutely necessary)
3.	**chemical**	*adj.* ▶	(related to the properties of substances)
4.	**properly**	*adv.* ▶	(correctly)
5.	**presence**	*n.* ▶	(the state of being in a place, of being present)
6.	**pigment**	*n.* ▶	(a substance that gives color to plant or animal tissues)
7.	**release**	*v.* ▶	(to let go)
8.	**recombine**	*v.* ▶	(to join together differently)
9.	**continuously**	*adv.* ▶	(without end)
10.	**existence**	*n.* ▶	(the state of existing or being)

TALLY [ ]   VOCABULARY **5**

Points

List 3: Word Relatives

	Verb	Noun	Adjective
Family 1	use (to employ for a purpose)	user usage	usable
Family 2	contain (to hold inside itself)	container	
Family 3	reverse (to change to the opposite)	reversal	reversible
Family 4	combine (to join together)	combination	
Family 5	structure (to arrange or to build)	structure	structural

(ACTIVITY B) *Spelling Dictation*

1.	**4.**
2.	**5.**
3.	**6.**

SPELLING   6
Points

ACTIVITY C *Passage Reading and Comprehension*

Note: For this activity, you will need Reproducible B found in the *Teacher's Guide*.

Plants

A

Many types of plants exist in the world. Plants cover much of the earth's
surface. All plants have leaves, but some plants have no flowers, stems, or roots.
Nevertheless, plants are essential to the existence of the earth's ecosystems. (#1)

Remember that all energy and matter that organisms require must be available
within their ecosystem. Just as protists and bacteria do, plants capture the sun's
energy and transform it into food energy (matter) for themselves and other
organisms. Plants are uniquely structured to make food from the sun's energy and
transform the food energy into usable food. In the next section, you will learn how
the plant's leaves are integral to the role that a plant plays in its ecosystem. (#2)

B

Photosynthesis in Plants

The job of the plant's leaves is to use light energy from the sun to make food
for the plant. This process is called **photosynthesis**. In the word photosynthesis,
the "photo" part of the process refers to this light energy being used to split the
molecules of water and carbon dioxide. The "synthesis" part refers to putting
things together, in this case putting molecules back together to make a sugar
called glucose. (#3)

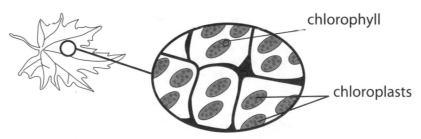

Photosynthesis occurs only in the presence of chlorophyll. Here's how it
works: Leaves contain little packets of green, chlorophyll pigment. These
packets, called **chloroplasts**, collect the sun's energy. The leaves then use this
light energy from the sun to split water (H_2O) already in the plant into hydrogen
and oxygen. The hydrogen stays in the plant, and the oxygen passes out of the
leaves and into the air around the plant. Next, the plant recombines the
hydrogen molecules (H_2) with carbon dioxide (CO_2) from the air to form a sugar
called **glucose** ($C_6H_{12}O_6$), an energy-rich food. The light energy is captured and
stored in the chemical bonds of the sugar molecule. In the next section on

Line numbers: 14, 28, 39, 51, 64, 76, 89, 104, 119, 122, 139, 151, 167, 179, 192, 194, 205, 215, 227, 242, 257, 270, 284, 297

311	cellular respiration, you will learn how the energy is released so that the plant
325	can use it. (#4)
328	Photosynthesis, or using light energy to transform water and carbon dioxide
339	into glucose sugar, happens every day. As a special waste product, molecules of
352	oxygen (O_2) are released into the air. What a special waste product it is! The
367	oxygen released by plants becomes part of the air we breathe. In fact, plants
381	provide earth with half of its oxygen! Microbes, members of the bacteria and
394	protist kingdoms, also photosynthesize and bring energy into ecosystems. These
404	microbes release the other half of the planet's oxygen. (#5)

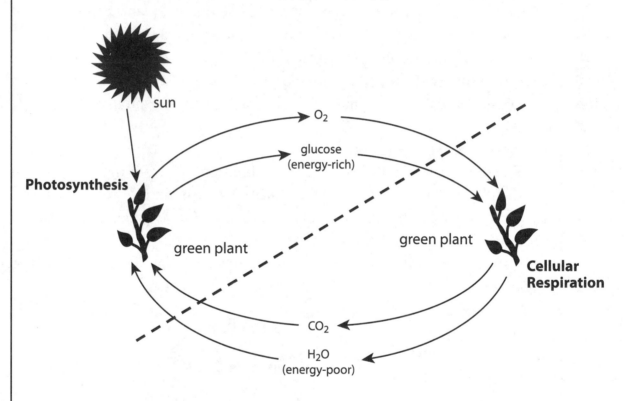

C

413	**Cellular Respiration in Plants**
417	**Cellular respiration** in plants is the energy-releasing process that is the
429	opposite of photosynthesis. During photosynthesis, plants release oxygen.
437	During cellular respiration, they take in oxygen. Even though plants have made
449	energy-rich food (glucose) during photosynthesis, they cannot access the energy
460	in the food unless they also take in oxygen from the air and release the energy.
476	By combining oxygen with the glucose they have made, they release a lot of
490	energy as well as carbon dioxide and water.
498	When plants combine oxygen from the air with food (glucose), the process of
511	photosynthesis is reversed and the stored energy originally gained from the sun
523	is released to power the plants and help them grow and continue to live. (#6)

D

537	**The Role of Plants in Ecosystems**
543	In order for each ecosystem to function properly, photosynthesis and cellular
554	respiration in plants are both essential. As a result of photosynthesis, plants
566	make their own food, and other organisms have enough oxygen to breathe. As a
580	result of cellular respiration, plants have energy for living and growing, plants
592	provide food for other organisms, and water and carbon dioxide are continuously
604	put back into the ecosystem for plants to use again. If plants had to use up
620	water, carbon dioxide, and oxygen without producing any, the ecosystem would
631	have used up these resources a long time ago. We will learn more about how
646	energy and matter move through ecosystems in the next article. (#7)
656	

(ACTIVITY D) *Fluency Building*

Cold Timing	[ ]	**Practice 1**	[ ]
Practice 2	[ ]	**Hot Timing**	[ ]

(ACTIVITY E) *Comprehension Questions—Multiple Choice*

Comprehension Strategy—Multiple Choice

Step 1: Read the item.
Step 2: Read all of the choices.
Step 3: Think about why each choice might be correct or incorrect. Check the article as needed.
Step 4: From the possible correct choices, select the best answer.

1. (Main idea) **If this article needed a new title, which of these would be the best?**
   a. The Parts of Plants
   b. Ecosystems: A Mix of Living and Nonliving Things
   c. The Importance of Plants to Ecosystems
   d. The Process of Photosynthesis

2. (Cause and effect) **The leaves are a very important plant structure because:**
   a. they provide shade for other organisms.
   b. they collect fresh water for insects.
   c. they use light energy to make food.
   d. they have sugar in them.

3. (Vocabulary) **The word "photosynthesis" contains two meaningful parts. Which best represents the meaning of "photosynthesis?"**
   a. picture + pull apart
   b. light + put together
   c. energy + parts
   d. camera + thesis

4. (Cause and effect) **If plants were always covered so sunlight could not reach the leaves, they would not survive because:**
   a. their roots would be unable to get water and minerals.
   b. no light energy would be available for the photosynthesis process.
   c. their leaves would wilt.
   d. too much oxygen would be released in the photosynthesis process.

MULTIPLE CHOICE COMPREHENSION | 4

(ACTIVITY F) *Vocabulary Activities*

Yes/No/Why

1. Is **chlorophyll essential**?

_____

_____

_____

_____

2. Is **carbon dioxide** a type of **glucose**?

_____

_____

_____

_____

3. Is our **existence** dependent upon **photosynthesis**?

_____

_____

_____

_____

Completion Activity

1. **combine:** to join together
   In order to make a great sandwich, you might combine

   _____

   _____

   _____

   _____

2. **essential:** absolutely necessary
   In order to drive a car, it is essential that you have

   _____

   _____

   _____

   _____

3. **continuously:** without end
   One example of an activity that goes on continuously is

   _____

   _____

   _____

   _____

4. **use:** to employ for a purpose
   Some of the things you use in class include

   _____

   _____

   _____

   _____

VOCABULARY 7

Points

(ACTIVITY G) *Expository Writing—Multi-Paragraph Answer*

Writing Strategy—Multi-Paragraph Answer

Step 1: LIST (List the details that are important enough to include in your answer.)

    Step 2: CROSS OUT (Reread the details. Cross out any that don't go with the topic.)

    Step 3: CONNECT (Connect any details that could go into one sentence.)

    Step 4: NUMBER (Number the details in a logical order.)

    Step 5: WRITE (Write the paragraph.)

Step 6: EDIT (Revise and proofread your answer.)

Prompt: Describe the two processes that plants perform to keep the energy cycle in ecosystems functioning.

Plan: Complete the Planning Box with your teacher.

Example Multi-Paragraph Plan

Planning Box
(topic a) *photosynthesis*
(detail) – *much of earth covered with plants*
(detail) – *process for making food*
(detail) – *leaves contain chloroplasts, which contain chlorophyll*
(detail) – *chloroplasts collect sun's energy*
(detail) – *light energy used to split water into hydrogen & oxygen*
(detail) – *hydrogen stays in plant*
(detail) – *oxygen leaves plant*
(detail) – *plant combines hydrogen with carbon dioxide from air to form glucose*
(detail) – *glucose is an energy-rich food*
(topic b) *cellular respiration*
(detail) – *process of releasing energy*
(detail) – *plants take in oxygen from air*
(detail) – *combine oxygen with glucose*
(detail) – *release energy & carbon dioxide & water*
(detail) – *stored energy powers the plant*
(detail) – *helps plants live and grow*

Write: Examine paragraph a. Then write paragraph b on a separate piece of paper.

Example Multi-Paragraph Answer

(paragraph a)

The first process that plants perform to keep the energy cycle in ecosystems functioning is photosynthesis. This is the plant's process for making food. The leaves in plants contain chloroplasts, which contain chlorophyll. These chloroplasts collect the sun's energy, which is used to split water into hydrogen and oxygen. The hydrogen stays in the plant while the oxygen leaves the plant. Next, the plant combines the hydrogen with carbon dioxide from the air to form glucose, an energy-rich food for the plant.

Evaluate: Evaluate the paragraphs using this rubric.

Rubric—Multi-Paragraph Answer	Student or Partner Rating	Teacher Rating
1. Did the author state the topic in the first sentence?	a. (Yes) Fix up b. Yes Fix up c. Yes Fix up	a. Yes No b. Yes No c. Yes No
2. Did the author include details that go with the topic?	a. (Yes) Fix up b. Yes Fix up c. Yes Fix up	a. Yes No b. Yes No c. Yes No
3. Did the author combine details in some of the sentences?	a. (Yes) Fix up b. Yes Fix up c. Yes Fix up	a. Yes No b. Yes No c. Yes No
4. Is the answer easy to understand?	Yes Fix up	Yes No
5. Did the author correctly spell words, particularly the words found in the article?	Yes Fix up	Yes No
6. Did the author use correct capitalization, capitalizing the first word in the sentence and proper names of people, places, and things?	Yes Fix up	Yes No
7. Did the author use correct punctuation, including a period at the end of each sentence?	Yes Fix up	Yes No

WRITING 13 Points

(ACTIVITY H) *Comprehension—Single-Paragraph Answer*

Writing Strategy—Single-Paragraph Answer

Step 1: Read the item.
Step 2: Turn the question into part of the answer and write it down.
Step 3: Think of the answer or locate the answer in the article.
Step 4: Complete your answer.

Prompt:

What is—Plants are organisms that transform the sun's energy into energy that is usable by them and other organisms.

What if—What would happen if plants couldn't use the sun's light energy to make food?

Write and Discuss: Write a paragraph. Then share your ideas. Use the Discussion Guidelines.

Discussion Guidelines

Speaker		Listener	
Looks like:	**Sounds like:**	**Looks like:**	**Sounds like:**
• Facing peers • Making eye contact • Participating	• Using pleasant, easy-to-hear voice • Sharing opinions, supporting facts and reasons from the article and from your experience • Staying on the topic	• Facing speaker • Making eye contact • Participating	• Waiting quietly to speak • Giving positive, supportive comments • Disagreeing respectfully

WRITING   DISCUSSION

4 Points   4 Points

(ACTIVITY A) *Vocabulary*

List 1: Tell

1. **chemosynthesis**   *n.* ▶ (the process by which certain organisms break down energy-rich molecules in order to make their own food)

2. **orca**   *n.* ▶ (a killer whale)

3. **alga**   *n.* ▶ (a simple, nonflowering plant that is usually found in or around water)

4. **algae**   *n.* ▶ (more than one alga; the plural of alga)

5. **lichens**   *n.* ▶ (slow-growing plants composed of algae and fungi)

6. **caribou**   *n.* ▶ (a type of reindeer living in northern Canada and in Alaska)

List 2: Strategy Practice

1. **producers**   *n.* ▶ (organisms that produce their own food)

2. **consumers**   *n.* ▶ (organisms that eat other organisms)

3. **decomposers**   *n.* ▶ (organisms that break down dead organisms)

4. **microscope**   *n.* ▶ (an instrument used to see very small things)

5. **microscopic**   *adj.* ▶ (so small as to be seen only with a microscope)

6. **recycling**   *v.* ▶ (changing waste to reusable items)

7. **arrangement**   *n.* ▶ (the result of being placed, or arranged, in a certain way)

8. **relatively**   *adv.* ▶ (in relation to something else; comparatively)

9. **mutual**   *adj.* ▶ (shared)

10. **parasite**   *n.* ▶ (an organism that lives in or on another organism and receives benefits while harming the other organism)

TALLY ☐   VOCABULARY ◺ **5**

Points   *Student Book: Application Lesson 3*   **39**

List 3: Word Relatives

	Verb	Noun	Adjective
Family 1	cycle (to occur over and over again in a definite order)	cycle	cyclic
Family 2	collect (to put together a group of things)	collection collector	collective
Family 3	reduce (to make smaller in number or size)	reduction reducer	reduced
Family 4	process (to go through a series of actions leading to an end, or to take a course of action)	process processor	
Family 5	require (to have need of)	requirement	

(ACTIVITY B) *Spelling Dictation*

1.		**4.**	
2.		**5.**	
3.		**6.**	

SPELLING 6

Points

ACTIVITY C *Passage Reading and Comprehension*

Note: For this activity, you will need Reproducible C found in the *Teacher's Guide*.

Energy and Matter Moving Through Ecosystems

A

13 | All living things in every ecosystem on earth need a constant supply of
26 | energy and matter to continue to live. Energy and matter constantly move or
36 | cycle through ecosystems. Plants and microscopic organisms such as bacteria
51 | and protists collect energy from the sun and use it to produce their own food.
63 | These **food producers** are then consumed by all other organisms, or **food**
73 | **consumers**. Finally, certain organisms, known as **decomposers**, break down dead
86 | and dying organic matter (matter that was once living) and return nutrients to
      | the soil for plants to use once again. (#1)

Food Producers

94 |
96 | Food producers don't need to consume other organisms in order to survive.
108 | They make their own food. Producers occupy all portions of the planet. Most
121 | producers are plants. Plants capture their energy from the sun and produce
133 | their own food through the process of photosynthesis. However, scientists have
144 | discovered that some organisms don't use sunlight as their energy source, yet
156 | they are still food producers. These producers break apart energy-rich
167 | molecules to produce their own food. This process of breaking apart simple
179 | molecules to harvest the energy is known as **chemosynthesis**. It is a process
192 | similar to photosynthesis, however these producers use the energy from
202 | chemicals instead of energy from the sun to produce food. (#2)

Photosynthesis
Energy from sun's light

Chemosynthesis
Energy from chemicals

sun

green plant

above ground (light)

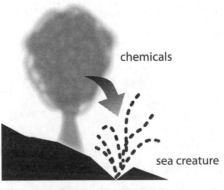

chemicals

sea creature

bottom of ocean (no light)

Sources of Energy for Food

B 212 | **The Energy Link Between the Sun and Ecosystems**
220 | Food producers have a critical role in all ecosystems. The producers that
232 | capture energy from the sun are the energy link between the sun and other
246 | living things. Producers capture energy from the sun and store that energy in
259 | food molecules in their own body structures. That energy then provides food for
272 | all other members of an ecosystem, including humans. Every living thing
283 | depends on producers for their food energy. Without producers, there would be
295 | no living things. The more producers in an ecosystem, the more the ecosystem
308 | is energy-rich, productive, and able to support a variety of living things. When
322 | producers are reduced in size and number, the richness and diversity of that
335 | ecosystem is also reduced. (#3)

C

339 | **Food Consumers**
341 | Food consumers are organisms that are unable to produce their own food.
353 | Essentially, any organism that eats another organism is a consumer. People are
365 | consumers because they consume products made from plants and animals.
375 | Birds, whales, spiders, and horses are consumers. Even smaller creatures,
385 | including the protists in water and in soil, are consumers. (#4)

D

395 | **The Energy Links Between Producers and Consumers**
402 | To show the energy links between producers and consumers, scientists
412 | created models called **food chains** and **food webs**. A food chain shows the flow
426 | of energy from a food producer to one consumer after another. In other words,
440 | a plant provides food for an organism, which provides food for another
452 | organism, and so on. In one example, a producer provides food for a herring,
466 | the herring is consumed by a salmon, the salmon is consumed by a sea lion, and
482 | the sea lion is consumed by an orca (killer whale). The illustration below shows
496 | another example, with the food producer at the base of the food chain.

509 | When food chains overlap, they form a food web. The term food web
522 | describes the complex feeding relationships that occur in most ecosystems. For
533 | example, in the ecosystem described above, whales consume sea lions and also
545 | consume other organisms. Sea lions eat salmon and also other organisms. So,
557 | several food chains overlap to create a marine life food web. (#5)

E	568	**Special Relationships in Ecosystems**
	572	The collection and transfer of food energy in an ecosystem does not always
	585	require organisms to die. Some energy transfers are relatively harmless.
	595	**Parasites** are organisms that get their food from living in, or on other organisms.
	609	Many animals, and even people, have parasites living in them. Parasites can be
	622	relatively harmless, or deadly. (#6)
	626	Some energy transfer relationships are friendly, such as those that occur with
	638	lichens. **Lichens** are mossy-looking things that grow on trees and rocks. Lichens
	651	are major producers in the food web of the tundra. They are consumed by
	665	caribou and lemmings, which are consumed by wolves. Lichens are actually two
	677	organisms, fungi and algae, living together and helping each other. The green
	689	alga of the lichen is a producer and a photosynthesizer. But, the alga needs
	703	water, minerals, and a place to live. The fungus, like mushrooms and mold,
	716	cannot produce. The fungus must consume. Fungi act like sponges, collecting
	727	water and nutrients and providing the living space that the algae need. In
	740	return, the fungi are rewarded with a supply of food from the algae. This special
	755	arrangement is a mutual community of two types of organisms. (#7)
F		
	765	**Recycling Energy and Matter**
	769	The last link of any food chain is an organism known as a decomposer.
	783	Decomposers break down and feed on dead organisms. Some fungi and bacteria
	795	are decomposers.
	797	Eventually, decomposers also die. But this isn't the end of the story, because
	810	there is no end. When decomposers die, the energy and nutrients contained in
	823	their bodies are released into the ecosystem and quickly taken up from the soil
	837	by producers (plants). Energy and matter are thus recycled again and again.
	849	This recycling is like a bicycle chain; all the links of the chain are connected, and
	865	the chain keeps going around and around. The last link connects to the first, and
	880	each link is important so that the system functions properly. (#8)
	890	

(ACTIVITY D) *Fluency Building*

Cold Timing [ ]   **Practice 1** [ ]

Practice 2 [ ]   **Hot Timing** [ ]

(ACTIVITY E) *Comprehension Questions—Multiple Choice*

Comprehension Strategy—Multiple Choice

Step 1: Read the item.

Step 2: Read all of the choices.

Step 3: Think about why each choice might be correct or incorrect. Check the article as needed.

Step 4: From the possible correct choices, select the best answer.

1. (Compare and contrast) **Select the statement that summarizes the most important difference between food producers and consumers.**

   a. Consumers are dependent on food producers.

   b. Food producers make their own food. Consumers must eat other organisms.

   c. Food producers are plants. Animals are consumers.

   d. Food producers are vast in number. Consumers are far fewer in number.

2. (Compare and contrast) **What is the essential difference between the process of photosynthesis and chemosynthesis?**

   a. In photosynthesis, energy is captured from the sun. In chemosynthesis, energy comes from the breaking apart of molecules.

   b. Photosynthesis occurs in plants. Chemosynthesis occurs in animals.

   c. Photosynthesis is a much more common process than chemosynthesis.

   d. Photosynthesis and chemosynthesis are both processes of producing food.

3. (Cause and effect) **Which of these is not an example of a food chain?**

   a. plant → bug → robin → cat

   b. plankton → herring → salmon → sea lion → whale

   c. grass → deer → wolf → vulture

   d. sheep → wolf → vulture

4. (Vocabulary) **"Microscopic" has two meaningful parts: "micro" and "scopic." What are the meanings of the parts?**

   a. small + view or see

   b. small + understanding

   c. loud + view or see

   d. loud + understanding

MULTIPLE CHOICE COMPREHENSION | 4

(ACTIVITY F) *Vocabulary Activities*

Yes/No/Why

1. Are **orcas producers**?

_____

_____

_____

_____

2. Are **caribou microscopic**?

_____

_____

_____

_____

3. Are **decomposers** necessary for **recycling**?

_____

_____

_____

_____

Completion Activities

1. **relatively:** in relation to something else; comparatively
Name three things you would like for your birthday that are relatively inexpensive.

_____

_____

_____

_____

2. **collect:** to put together a group of things
People collect all types of objects, such as

_____

_____

_____

_____

3. **requirement:** a need
One of the requirements for getting a driver's license is

_____

_____

_____

_____

4. **mutual:** shared
My friend and I have a mutual interest in

_____

_____

_____

_____

VOCABULARY 7

Points

(ACTIVITY G) *Expository Writing—Multi-Paragraph Answer*

Writing Strategy—Multi-Paragraph Answer

Step 1: LIST (List the details that are important enough to include in your answer.)

    Step 2: CROSS OUT (Reread the details. Cross out any that don't go with the topic.)

    Step 3: CONNECT (Connect any details that could go into one sentence.)

    Step 4: NUMBER (Number the details in a logical order.)

    Step 5: WRITE (Write the paragraph.)

Step 6: EDIT (Revise and proofread your answer.)

Prompt: Explain the roles of producers, consumers, and decomposers in the transfer of energy within an ecosystem.

Plan: Complete the Planning Box with your teacher.

Example Multi-Paragraph Plan

Planning Box
(topic a) *producers*
(detail) – *photosynthesis—plants capture energy from sun to make food*
(detail) – *chemosynthesis—produce food by breaking apart molecules to capture energy*
(detail) – *producers provide food for other organisms*
(detail) – *energy link between sun and other living things*
(detail) – *without producers, no life*
(detail) – *consumers eat consumers*
(topic b) *consumers*
(detail) – *unable to produce their own food by capturing the sun's energy*
(detail) – *an organism that eats another organism is a consumer*
(detail) – *consumers eat producers*
(detail) – *in food webs consumers also eat consumers*
(detail) – *gain energy needed for life*
(topic c) *decomposers*
(detail) – *plants are producers*
(detail) – *decomposers break down and feed on dead organisms*
(detail) – *when decomposers die, energy released into ecosystem*
(detail) – *when decomposers die, nutrients released into ecosystem*
(detail) – *plants can then take energy and nutrients from soil*

Write: Examine paragraph a and write paragraphs b and c on a separate piece of paper.

Example Multi-Paragraph Answer

(paragraph a)

   The role of producers in the ecosystem is to make food for themselves and other organisms. In the process of photosynthesis, plants capture energy from the sun to produce their own food. In a similar process, chemosynthesis, organisms use energy from the breaking apart of molecules to produce food. Producers provide food for other organisms. As a result, producers are the energy link between the sun and all living organisms. Without producers, there would be no life.

Evaluate: Evaluate the paragraphs using this rubric.

Rubric— Multi-Paragraph Answer	Student or Partner Rating	Teacher Rating
1. Did the author state the topic in the first sentence?	a. (Yes) Fix up b. Yes Fix up c. Yes Fix up	a. Yes No b. Yes No c. Yes No
2. Did the author include details that go with the topic?	a. (Yes) Fix up b. Yes Fix up c. Yes Fix up	a. Yes No b. Yes No c. Yes No
3. Did the author combine details in some of the sentences?	a. (Yes) Fix up b. Yes Fix up c. Yes Fix up	a. Yes No b. Yes No c. Yes No
4. Is the answer easy to understand?	Yes Fix up	Yes No
5. Did the author correctly spell words, particularly the words found in the article?	Yes Fix up	Yes No
6. Did the author use correct capitalization, capitalizing the first word in the sentence and proper names of people, places, and things?	Yes Fix up	Yes No
7. Did the author use correct punctuation, including a period at the end of each sentence?	Yes Fix up	Yes No

WRITING 13 *Points*

3

ACTIVITY H — *Comprehension—Single-Paragraph Answer*

Writing Strategy—Single-Paragraph Answer

Step 1: Read the item.
Step 2: Turn the question into part of the answer and write it down.
Step 3: Think of the answer or locate the answer in the article.
Step 4: Complete your answer.

Prompt:

What Is—Producers, consumers, and decomposers live together in an ecosystem and use existing resources to keep energy and matter moving through the ecosystem.

What If—What would happen if, all of a sudden, decomposers could no longer do their job?

Write and Discuss: Write a paragraph. Then share your ideas. Use the Discussion Guidelines.

Discussion Guidelines

Speaker		Listener	
Looks like:	**Sounds like:**	**Looks like:**	**Sounds like:**
• Facing peers • Making eye contact • Participating	• Using pleasant, easy-to-hear voice • Sharing opinions, supporting facts and reasons from the article and from your experience • Staying on the topic	• Facing speaker • Making eye contact • Participating	• Waiting quietly to speak • Giving positive, supportive comments • Disagreeing respectfully

WRITING   DISCUSSION

4 Points   4 Points

ACTIVITY A *Vocabulary*

List 1: Tell

1.	ancient	*adj.* ▶	(old)
2.	dehydration	*n.* ▶	(the loss of water from an organism)
3.	elements	*n.* ▶	(basic parts from which something is made)
4.	ingredients	*n.* ▶	(the foods or other elements combined to make a mixture)
5.	Louis Pasteur	*n.* ▶	(the scientist who discovered how to keep foods safe by killing microbes with heat)
6.	pasteurization	*n.* ▶	(the process of using heat to kill microbes and prevent food from spoiling rapidly)
7.	pathogens	*n.* ▶	(microorganisms, such as bacteria and viruses, that cause disease)
8.	sodium benzoate	*n.* ▶	(an odorless white powder used to keep food fresh)
9.	sulfur dioxide	*n.* ▶	(a colorless liquid used to keep food fresh)
10.	techniques	*n.* ▶	(particular methods of doing things)
11.	vinegar	*n.* ▶	(a sour liquid used to keep food from spoiling)

List 2: Strategy Practice

1.	alternatives	*n.* ▶	(things used or things done instead of other things)
2.	contaminated	*v.* ▶	(spoiled)
3.	controversy	*n.* ▶	(a longstanding disagreement)
4.	deprive	*v.* ▶	(to take away from)
5.	environments	*n.* ▶	(the physical surroundings)
6.	nutritional	*adj.* ▶	(having to do with food so the body functions properly)
7.	poisonous	*adj.* ▶	(causing death or illness if put into the body)
8.	refrigeration	*n.* ▶	(the process used to make things cool or cold)
9.	spoilage	*n.* ▶	(the decay of food)
10.	sterilization	*n.* ▶	(the act of making something free from bacteria)

TALLY ☐   **VOCABULARY** **5**

Points

List 3: Word Relatives

	Verb	Noun	Adjective
Family 1	preserve (to keep safe or free from harm)	preservation preservative	preservable
Family 2	survive (to live longer than)	survivor survival	
Family 3	research (to study or investigate in a particular field	researcher	researchable
Family 4	moisten (to make or become slightly wet)	moisture	moist
Family 5	conduct (to direct)	conduction conductor	

ACTIVITY B *Spelling Dictation*

1.	**4.**
2.	**5.**
3.	**6.**

SPELLING

6

Points

(ACTIVITY C) *Passage Reading and Comprehension*

Note: For this activity, you will need Reproducible D found in the *Teacher's Guide*.

Food Preservation

A

13
28
Have you ever seen food that has become moldy? Have you ever tasted spoiled milk? Maybe you bit into part of an apple that was mushy and brown. These are some of the examples of what can happen when food spoils.

41
Spoiled Food

43
53
67
79
Food spoils because microscopic organisms, or **microbes**, called bacteria and fungi, break down or change the structure of the food. These microbes are the most common cause of food poisoning, a condition that frequently results in mild illness for a short period but occasionally results in extreme illness.

91
107
121
134
In order to avoid spoilage, you must find a way to kill the microbes, to slow down their growth, or to change the composition of the food so microbes can't use it anymore. Many food preservation techniques can be utilized to keep food from spoiling. (#1)

B

136
Drying and Smoking

139
151
164
The most ancient form of food preservation is simply drying or dehydrating the food. Dehydration deprives the microbes of one of their basic needs, which is water. Just like you and plants, microbes can't live without water. (#2)

176
192
206
One way to dry out the food is to add large amounts of salt. Not many organisms can survive living in salty environments. Thus, salt curing of food is an effective way to prevent, or slow, the growth of microbes.

216
228
241
257
272
Smoking is used to preserve meat and fish. Smoke contains chemicals that are toxic, or poisonous, to microbes. Smoke also creates a sort of waterproofing. When meat is hung over a small, cold, smoky fire for a number of days, the meat dries and takes on a coating of smoke that protects it from moisture and from rotting. (#3)

C

274
Refrigeration and Freezing

277
289
298
315
330
Today, the most widely used forms of food preservation are refrigeration and freezing. Refrigeration slows microbial action. Refrigerated food items might stay good for a week or two, instead of spoiling in a day. Freezing can slow or stop the growth of microbes, which is why things can be stored in a freezer for a long time. Refrigeration and freezing are popular methods for

| 342 | preserving food because they change the taste, texture, and nutritional content |
| 353 | of the food items very little. (#4) |

D

359	**Canning, Pasteurization, and Pickling**
363	Canned and pickled foods can last a very long time. Before people had
376	refrigerators and freezers in their homes, they often canned and pickled
387	vegetables to eat during the winter months. All food contains bacteria and does
400	not last very long without sterilizing or sealing it. In the canning process, food is
415	boiled in the can or jar. This boiling kills all present microbes and seals the
430	container so that no new microbes can get in. The food is then sterile, or free
446	from living microbes, until the can is opened. This heat sterilization method is
459	also known as **pasteurization**, named after its founder, Louis Pasteur. In addition
471	to killing the microbes outright, the sealed cans also deprive the microbes of
484	another essential of life, which is air. Canned foods have a long shelf life, but the
500	nutritional content, taste, and texture of the food is often very different from the
514	fresh version. (#5)

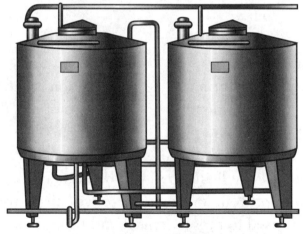

Pasteurization Equipment

516	Pickling combines salt with an acid, like vinegar, or a base, like baking soda.
530	Acids, bases, and salt create an unfriendly environment for the microbes. People
542	used to pickle fruits, vegetables, and meats; however, because the taste changes
554	so much when pickled, pickling is now used mainly for pickles, not as a means of
570	food preservation. (#6)

E

572	**Chemical Preservatives**
574	Plants often produce chemicals that are toxic to other organisms. What is
586	poisonous to you may not be poisonous to a squirrel or to a microbe. Spices are
602	made from parts of plants. Some spices, used in large amounts, can slow the

616
629 growth of microbes because of the chemicals they produce. In the past, spices, such as curry, ginger, and cayenne pepper, were often used to preserve foods.

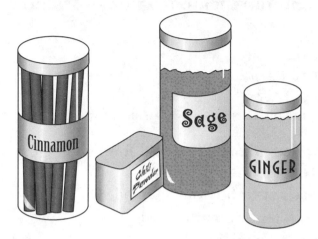

642
654
665
676
689 Other chemicals are added to foods as preservatives. If you read the ingredients of some favorite foods, you may find that common chemical preservatives like sulfur dioxide, sodium benzoate, or sodium nitrite have been added. Some foods with chemical preservatives may have a shelf life of several years.

690
700
712
725
737 Although chemical preservatives are useful, there is some controversy about their use. Some people are severely allergic to nitrites and other preservatives. Other people feel that adding any chemicals to food diminishes its safety and nutrition. Because of this controversy, more research is being conducted to find natural alternatives that prevent food from spoiling. (#7)

F

744 **Importance of Food Preservation**
748
758
769
781
793
806 Besides preserving the taste and nutrition of food, preservation techniques also protect people from food-borne pathogens. Pathogens are harmful bacteria that spread to people when they eat contaminated food. Some food-borne illnesses are quite serious and can be life threatening. The food preservation techniques discussed here, as well as others, help ensure that the food supply remains safe and healthy for everyone. (#8)

812

ACTIVITY D Fluency Building

Cold Timing [ ]   Practice 1 [ ]

Practice 2 [ ]   Hot Timing [ ]

ACTIVITY E *Comprehension Questions—Multiple Choice*

Comprehension Strategy—Multiple Choice

Step 1: Read the item.
Step 2: Read all of the choices.
Step 3: Think about why each choice might be correct or incorrect. Check the article as needed.
Step 4: From the possible correct choices, select the best answer.

1. (Cause and effect) **If you wanted to avoid food spoilage, which of these methods would you NOT use?**
   a. Picking out each microbe from the food.
   b. Killing the microbes within the food.
   c. Slowing down the growth of the microbes.
   d. Changing the composition of the food so microbes can't use it.

2. (Compare and contrast) **How do "drying" and "smoking" methods of preservation differ?**
   a. Drying is a method of preserving plant foods. Smoking is a method of preserving meat.
   b. Drying removes water from the food, depriving microbes of a necessity. Smoking not only dries the food, but the smoke is toxic to the microbes.
   c. Drying is an ancient form of preservation. Smoking is a recent development in preservation.
   d. Drying always requires the use of salt to kill microbes. Smoking requires the use of fire to make the meat or fish poisonous.

3. (Compare and contrast) **How do canning and pickling preservation processes differ?**
   a. Canned foods have a long shelf life due to the killing of microbes. Pickled foods have a short shelf life due to the growth of microbes in the acid.
   b. Canned foods taste like fresh vegetables. Pickled foods have an altered flavor.
   c. In the canning process, the food is boiled in a can or jar and the microbes are killed. In pickling, ingredients such as salt or vinegar are added to the foods to create a "hostile" environment for microbes.
   d. Canned foods are in cans. Pickled foods are in jars.

4. (Main idea) **If you were picking a clever title for this article, which of the following would most accurately convey the article's topic?**
   a. Spice is NICE
   b. Don't Preserve—SERVE
   c. DRY, FRY, Then CRY
   d. Microbes BEWARE!

MULTIPLE CHOICE COMPREHENSION

ACTIVITY F Vocabulary Activities

Yes/No/Why

1. Could **ingredients** be **poisonous**?

_____

_____

_____

_____

2. Is **pasteurization** the same process as **refrigeration**?

_____

_____

_____

_____

3. Are there good **alternatives** to **controversy**?

_____

_____

_____

_____

Completion Activities

1. **dehydration:** the loss of water from an organism
   You might experience dehydration if you

   _____

   _____

   _____

   _____

2. **research:** to study or investigate in a particular field
   During my lifetime, I hope we have research on

   _____

   _____

   _____

   _____

3. **deprive:** to take away from
   If you stay out past your curfew, your parents might deprive you of

   _____

   _____

   _____

   _____

4. **preserved:** kept safe or free from harm
   Berries and other fruits are often preserved by

   _____

   _____

   _____

   _____

VOCABULARY 7

Points

ACTIVITY G *Expository Writing—Multi-Paragraph Answer*

Writing Strategy—Multi-Paragraph Answer

Step 1: LIST (List the details that are important enough to include in your answer.)

Step 2: CROSS OUT (Reread the details. Cross out any that don't go with the topic.)

Step 3: CONNECT (Connect any details that could go into one sentence.)

Step 4: NUMBER (Number the details in a logical order.)

Step 5: WRITE (Write the paragraph.)

Step 6: EDIT (Revise and proofread your answer.)

Prompt: Describe the three most popular types of food preservation methods used today.

Plan: Complete the Planning Box with your teacher.

Example Multi-Paragraph Plan

Planning Box
(topic a) **refrigeration & freezing**
(detail) **– slows or stops growth of microbes**
(detail) **– stays good for weeks rather than days**
(detail) **– doesn't change taste, texture, or nutritional content**
(topic b) **canning & pasteurization**
(detail) **– food boiled in can or jar**
(detail) **– boiling kills microbes**
(detail) **– freezing slows growth of microbes**
(detail) **– container sealed so microbes can't enter**
(detail) **– long shelf life**
(detail) **– nutritional content, taste, & texture altered**
(topic c) **chemical preservation**
(detail)
(detail)
(detail)
(detail)
(detail)
(detail)

Write: Examine paragraph a and write paragraphs b and c on a separate piece of paper.

Example Multi-Paragraph Answer

(paragraph a)

Refrigeration and freezing are popular modern means of food preservation. These processes result in slowing down or stopping the growth of microbes in food. As a result, the food may last weeks rather than days. These methods are also popular because they don't change the taste, texture, or nutritional value of the food very much.

Evaluate: Evaluate the paragraphs using this rubric.

Rubric— Multi-Paragraph Answer	Student or Partner Rating	Teacher Rating
1. Did the author state the topic in the first sentence?	a. (Yes) Fix up b. Yes Fix up c. Yes Fix up	a. Yes No b. Yes No c. Yes No
2. Did the author include details that go with the topic?	a. (Yes) Fix up b. Yes Fix up c. Yes Fix up	a. Yes No b. Yes No c. Yes No
3. Did the author combine details in some of the sentences?	a. (Yes) Fix up b. Yes Fix up c. Yes Fix up	a. Yes No b. Yes No c. Yes No
4. Is the answer easy to understand?	Yes Fix up	Yes No
5. Did the author correctly spell words, particularly the words found in the article?	Yes Fix up	Yes No
6. Did the author use correct capitalization, capitalizing the first word in the sentence and proper names of people, places, and things?	Yes Fix up	Yes No
7. Did the author use correct punctuation, including a period at the end of each sentence?	Yes Fix up	Yes No

WRITING 13
Points

ACTIVITY H *Comprehension—Single-Paragraph Answer*

Writing Strategy—Single-Paragraph Answer

Step 1: Read the item.
Step 2: Turn the question into part of the answer and write it down.
Step 3: Think of the answer or locate the answer in the article.
Step 4: Complete your answer.

Prompt:

What Is–We depend on our food supply to be available, varied, and fresh.

What If–What would happen if all known methods of food preservation were suddenly ineffective in stopping the growth of microbes?

Write and Discuss: Write a paragraph. Then share your ideas. Use the Discussion Guidelines.

Discussion Guidelines

Speaker		Listener	
Looks like:	**Sounds like:**	**Looks like:**	**Sounds like:**
• Facing peers • Making eye contact • Participating	• Using pleasant, easy-to-hear voice • Sharing opinions, supporting facts and reasons from the article and from your experience • Staying on the topic	• Facing speaker • Making eye contact • Participating	• Waiting quietly to speak • Giving positive, supportive comments • Disagreeing respectfully

WRITING   DISCUSSION

4   4

Points   *Points*

(ACTIVITY A) *Vocabulary*

List 1: Tell

1. **arteries**   *n.* ▸ (large blood vessels that carry blood away from the heart)

2. **arterioles**   *n.* ▸ (small blood vessels that carry blood away from the heart)

3. **arteriosclerosis**   *n.* ▸ (a condition that happens when the walls of the arteries become thick and not as flexible)

4. **plaque**   *n.* ▸ (a hard substance that builds up in blood vessels and limits the flow of blood)

5. **atherosclerosis**   *n.* ▸ (a condition that happens when deposits of plaque build up on the inside of the arteries)

6. **atria**   *n.* ▸ (the two top chambers of the heart)

7. **capillaries**   *n.* ▸ (small blood vessels that connect arteries to venules)

8. **deoxygenated**   *v.* ▸ (having the oxygen removed)

9. **hemoglobin**   *n.* ▸ (a substance in red blood cells that helps carry oxygen throughout the body)

10. **platelets**   *n.* ▸ (pieces of cells that prevent blood clotting)

11. **pulmonary**   *adj.* ▸ (relating to or affecting the lungs)

12. **systemic**   *adj.* ▸ (relating to or affecting the body)

13. **ventricles**   *n.* ▸ (the two lower chambers of the heart)

14. **venules**   *n.* ▸ (small blood vessels that connect capillaries to veins)

List 2: Strategy Practice

1. **cardiovascular**   *adj.* ▸ (of the body system that consists of the heart, blood, and blood vessels)

2. **circulates**   *v.* ▸ (moves from place to place in a circular path)

3. **components**   *n.* ▸ (parts)

4. **fragments**   *n.* ▸ (small pieces)

5. **infections**   *n.* ▸ (diseases caused by germs entering part of the body)

6. **multicellular**   *adj.* ▸ (made up of many cells)

7. **particular**   *adj.* ▸ (special)

8. **pressures**   *n.* ▸ (forces made by one thing against another)

9. **responsible for**   *adj.* ▸ (in charge of; charged with being the source for)

10. **trillion**   *n.* ▸ (the number 1 followed by 12 zeroes; a lot)

TALLY ☐   VOCABULARY 5

List 3: Word Relatives

	Verb	Noun	Adjective
Family 1	organize (to assemble to perform a specific function)	organization organizer	organizational
Family 2	transport (to carry from one place to another)	transportation	transportable
Family 3	promote (to encourage or assist in growth or development)	promotion promoter	promotional
Family 4	avoid (to keep away from)	avoidance	avoidable
Family 5	specialize (to adapt to a special job or function)	specialization	

(ACTIVITY B) *Spelling Dictation*

1.	4.
2.	5.
3.	6.

SPELLING **6**

Points

ACTIVITY C *Passage Reading and Comprehension*

Note: For this activity, you will need Reproducible E found in the *Teacher's Guide*.

The Cardiovascular System

A

15   All living things are made up of cells, the basic units of life. Most organisms
28 are made up of many, many cells (multicellular organisms). In fact, humans have
39 over a trillion cells. In multicellular organisms, various life functions are
52 performed by specialized groups of cells. In humans, there are five levels of
63 organization: cells, tissues, organs, organ systems, and the whole organism. **Cells**
75 group together to form **tissues**. Similar tissues group together to form **organs**,
88 and organs group together with other organs to form **organ systems**. Each organ
93 system performs a particular function. (#1)

104   One organ system is the **cardiovascular system**, which includes your heart,
117 blood, and blood vessels. This system is a type of transportation system that
128 delivers oxygen and nutrients throughout the body and then removes waste
140 products from the body. The cardiovascular system is one of several organ
154 systems that are central to the human body's functioning. For a person's body to
164 function smoothly, all organ systems, including the cardiovascular system, must
    run smoothly. (#2)

B

166 **The Heart**

168   Make a fist. Your **heart** is a muscle about the same size as your closed fist. It
185 is hollow on the inside and divided into four chambers, or parts. The top
199 chambers are the atria. The lower chambers are the ventricles. The atria pump
212 blood into the heart and down into the ventricles. The ventricles pump the
225 blood out of the heart and toward the rest of the body. When the blood goes
241 from the atria to the ventricles, it passes through valves that prevent the blood
255 from flowing backwards. (#3)

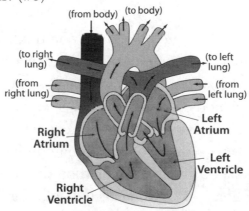

C

258 **The Blood**

260   Your blood is made up of liquid components (plasma) and solid components
272 (red blood cells, white blood cells, and platelets). The **plasma** is the liquid that
286 helps transport the solid parts of the blood from one part of the body to another.
302 Plasma is mostly water but also contains proteins, vitamins, minerals, and other
314 elements. (#4)

315   Your blood contains about 99 red blood cells for each white blood cell. The
329 red blood cells contain a substance called **hemoglobin**. With the help of the
342 hemoglobin, the red blood cells carry oxygen to all parts of the body. The
356 hemoglobin helps the cells hold the oxygen until it is delivered to places in the
371 body that need it. (#5)

375   The white blood cells are your body's best defense against infections or
387 disease. They work hard to destroy the foreign particles that cause sickness, such
400 as viruses or bacteria. The white blood cells use the cardiovascular system to
413 travel to the site of the infection. (#6)

420   **Platelets** are fragments, or pieces, of cells. They stick to the walls of the
434 blood vessels and help to promote clotting when a blood vessel is damaged.
447 Clotting helps stop bleeding and keeps blood from leaving the blood vessel. (#7)

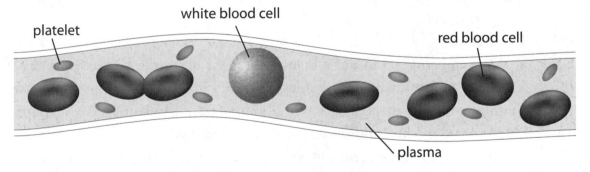

Components Found in the Blood

D

459 **Blood Pathways**

461   Your blood vessels move blood between the heart and other areas of the
474 body. Blood circulates throughout your body via two pathways: the systemic and
486 the pulmonary. The systemic pathway carries oxygen-rich blood from your heart
498 to all parts of your body except your lungs, and releases the oxygen and picks up
514 carbon dioxide. Then, it returns the deoxygenated blood back to your heart. The
527 pulmonary pathway carries the deoxygenated blood from your heart to your
538 lungs where the blood releases the carbon dioxide and picks up oxygen before
551 returning to the heart, where the cycle begins again. (#8)

E

560	**The Blood Vessels**
563	Your blood vessels include several types: arteries, arterioles, capillaries, veins,
573	and venules. **Arteries** are the largest type of blood vessel. The walls of the
587	arteries are thick and elastic so that blood can be carried at high pressures. As
602	they move away from the heart, they branch out into smaller blood vessels
615	called **arterioles**. Both arteries and arterioles are responsible for carrying blood
626	away from the heart. The blood eventually passes into tiny blood vessels called
639	**capillaries**. Capillaries link arteries to **veins** and provide an exchange point for
651	nutrients and waste. The capillaries are connected to veins by **venules**. The veins
664	are larger blood vessels that carry blood toward the heart. Blood traveling
676	through veins is much darker than blood in the arteries because the oxygen has
690	been removed and waste materials are present. (#9)

F

697	**Problems With the System**
701	Several diseases cause the cardiovascular system to stop working properly.
711	People with high blood pressure have narrowed blood vessels. This condition
722	makes the heart muscle work harder in order to get enough oxygen to other
736	parts of the body, which can damage the muscle or cause it to fail altogether.
751	Another problem, arteriosclerosis, happens when the walls of the arteries
761	become thick and not as flexible. Again, the heart must work too hard to send
776	the blood to other parts of the body. Finally, deposits called **plaque** build up on
791	the inside walls of the arteries and cause atherosclerosis. These deposits build
803	up because of smoking, poor diet, or high blood pressure. The heart cannot
816	pump the blood past the deposits, causing heart failure or stroke.

827	**Conclusion**
828	As you can see, your cardiovascular system is critical to your life vitality.
841	Fortunately, through a nutritional diet, avoidance of smoking, and daily exercise,
852	you can safeguard your own cardiovascular system. (#10)
859	

(ACTIVITY D) *Fluency Building*

Cold Timing	[ ]	**Practice 1**	[ ]
Practice 2	[ ]	**Hot Timing**	[ ]

(ACTIVITY E) *Comprehension Questions—Multiple Choice*

Comprehension Strategy—Multiple Choice

Step 1: Read the item.

Step 2: Read all of the choices.

Step 3: Think about why each choice might be correct or incorrect. Check the article as needed.

Step 4: From the possible correct choices, select the best answer.

1. (Main idea) **Which list best represents the levels of organization of human cells?**

    a. cells, organs, organ systems, tissue, whole human

    b. tissues, organs, organ systems, whole human

    c. cells, tissues, organs, organ systems, whole human

    d. heart, blood, blood vessels, arteries

2. (Vocabulary) **In the article, the author calls the cardiovascular system a "transportation system" because**

    a. like other transportation systems, it carries things from place to place.

    b. blood vessels and arteries are like the tunnels that trains pass through.

    c. like other transportation systems, it has a number of critical parts.

    d. the blood flows similarly to cars moving down a freeway.

3. (Cause and effect) **Determine which relationship is NOT true.**

    a. If you had an absence of hemoglobin, your body would have difficulty carrying oxygen to all parts of your body.

    b. If your body had an infection, red blood cells (the body's defense against infection) would travel to the infection.

    c. If your body had a reduced number of platelets in the blood, clotting would be impaired.

    d. If your blood vessels became narrow, you would have high blood pressure.

4. (Compare and contrast) **If you were comparing red and white blood cells, which of the following would be true of BOTH?**

    a. We have about the same number of red and white blood cells.

    b. Red and white blood cells work to destroy particles causing illness.

    c. Plasma carries red and white blood cells from one part of your body to another.

    d. Red and white blood cells contain hemoglobin which helps them deliver oxygen to all parts of the body.

MULTIPLE CHOICE COMPREHENSION

Points

(ACTIVITY F) *Vocabulary Activities*

Yes/No/Why

1. Does the **pulmonary** pathway include **ventricles**?

_____

_____

_____

_____

2. Do **arteries** lead to **infections**?

_____

_____

_____

_____

3. Can **plaque** be **responsible for** disease?

_____

_____

_____

_____

Completion Activities

1. **avoidance:** the act of keeping away from
   Things that you have an avoidance for include

   _____

   _____

   _____

   _____

2. **components:** parts
   The components of the perfect sound system include

   _____

   _____

   _____

   _____

3. **promotional:** having to do with encouragement or assistance in growth or development
   Businesses may have a promotional offer for their products. Some of these offers
   might be

   _____

   _____

   _____

   _____

4. **transportation:** something that carries things from one place to another
   Name six methods of transportation.

   _____

   _____

   _____

   _____

VOCABULARY **7**

(ACTIVITY G) *Expository Writing—Multi-Paragraph Answer*

Writing Strategy—Multi-Paragraph Answer

Step 1: LIST (List the details that are important enough to include in your answer.)

Step 2: CROSS OUT (Reread the details. Cross out any that don't go with the topic.)

Step 3: CONNECT (Connect any details that could go into one sentence.)

Step 4: NUMBER (Number the details in a logical order.)

Step 5: WRITE (Write the paragraph.)

Step 6: EDIT (Revise and proofread your answer.)

Prompt: Describe the structure and function of the three main parts of the cardiovascular system.

Plan: Complete the Planning Box with your teacher.

Example Multi-Paragraph Plan

Planning Box
(topic a) *heart*
(detail) – *4 chambers*
(detail) – *top chambers—atria*
(detail) – *bottom chambers—ventricles*
(detail) – *atria pumps blood into heart and down into ventricles*
(detail) – *ventricles pump blood out of the heart to rest of body*
(topic b) *blood*
(detail) – *made of liquid and solid components*
(detail) – *liquid component called plasma*
(detail) – *solid components include red blood cells, white blood cells, &*
platelets
(detail) – *plasma mostly water with proteins, vitamins, & minerals*
(detail) – *red blood cells carry oxygen to all parts of body*
(detail) – *white blood cells fight infection and diseases*
(detail) – *platelets help promote blood clotting*
(topic c) *blood vessels*
(detail)
(detail)
(detail)
(detail)
(detail)
(detail)
(detail)

Write: Examine paragraph a and write paragraphs b and c on a separate piece of paper.

Example Multi-Paragraph Answer

(paragraph a)

The heart is one part of the cardiovascular system. The heart has four chambers: two chambers on the top called the atria and two chambers on the bottom called the ventricles. The atria pump blood into the heart and then into the ventricles. Then, the ventricles pump blood out of the heart into the rest of the body.

Evaluate: Evaluate the paragraphs using this rubric.

Rubric— Multi-Paragraph Answer	Student or Partner Rating	Teacher Rating
1. Did the author state the topic in the first sentence?	a. (Yes) Fix up b. Yes Fix up c. Yes Fix up	a. Yes No b. Yes No c. Yes No
2. Did the author include details that go with the topic?	a. (Yes) Fix up b. Yes Fix up c. Yes Fix up	a. Yes No b. Yes No c. Yes No
3. Did the author combine details in some of the sentences?	a. (Yes) Fix up b. Yes Fix up c. Yes Fix up	a. Yes No b. Yes No c. Yes No
4. Is the answer easy to understand?	Yes Fix up	Yes No
5. Did the author correctly spell words, particularly the words found in the article?	Yes Fix up	Yes No
6. Did the author use correct capitalization, capitalizing the first word in the sentence and proper names of people, places, and things?	Yes Fix up	Yes No
7. Did the author use correct punctuation, including a period at the end of each sentence?	Yes Fix up	Yes No

5

(ACTIVITY H) *Comprehension—Single-Paragraph Answer*

Writing Strategy—Single-Paragraph Answer

Step 1: Read the item.
Step 2: Turn the question into part of the answer and write it down.
Step 3: Think of the answer or locate the answer in the article.
Step 4: Complete your answer.

Prompt:

What Is–A healthy cardiovascular system is critical to a person's overall health.

What If–What would happen to you and your daily activities if your white blood cells were weakened or destroyed?

Write and Discuss: Write a paragraph. Then share your ideas. Use the Discussion Guidelines.

Discussion Guidelines

Speaker		Listener	
Looks like:	**Sounds like:**	**Looks like:**	**Sounds like:**
• Facing peers • Making eye contact • Participating	• Using pleasant, easy-to-hear voice • Sharing opinions, supporting facts and reasons from the article and from your experience • Staying on the topic	• Facing speaker • Making eye contact • Participating	• Waiting quietly to speak • Giving positive, supportive comments • Disagreeing respectfully

WRITING   **DISCUSSION**

4   4

Points   *Points*

(ACTIVITY A) *Vocabulary*

List 1: Tell

1. **patients**   *n.*   ▶ (people under a doctor's care)
2. **medicines**   *n.*   ▶ (drugs or other substances used to treat disease or to relieve pain)
3. **procedure**   *n.*   ▶ (a course of action with steps in a definite order)
4. **recipient**   *n.*   ▶ (a person who receives)
5. **anesthetic**   *n.*   ▶ (a drug or other substance that causes loss of feeling, especially pain)
6. **efficiently**   *adv.* ▶ (getting the desired result with as little effort as possible)
7. **foreign**   *adj.* ▶ (not belonging to)

List 2: Strategy Practice

1. **generosity**   *n.*   ▶ (willingness to give or share freely)
2. **incompatible**   *adj.* ▶ (not able to work together or get along with)
3. **suitable**   *adj.* ▶ (meets the requirements of)
4. **surgery**   *n.*   ▶ (the removal or repair of injured or diseased parts of the body)
5. **suture**   *v.*   ▶ (to stitch together the edges of a cut or wound)
6. **consciousness**   *n.*   ▶ (the state of being awake)
7. **susceptible**   *adj.* ▶ (easily affected)
8. **immune**   *adj.* ▶ (protected from a disease or infection)
9. **medications**   *n.*   ▶ (substances used to treat diseases)
10. **gradually**   *adv.* ▶ (little by little; slowly)

TALLY [　　　]   VOCABULARY 5
Points

List 3: Word Relatives

	Verb	Noun	Adjective
Family 1	incorporate (to make part of another thing)	incorporation	incorporated
Family 2	designate (to indicate)	designation	
Family 3	permit (to allow)	permission	permissible
Family 4	donate (to give)	donor donation	
Family 5	commune (to come together)	community	communal

ACTIVITY B *Spelling Dictation*

1.	4.
2.	5.
3.	6.

(ACTIVITY C) *Passage Reading and Comprehension*

Note: For this activity, you will need Reproducible F found in the *Teacher's Guide*.

Heart Transplants

A

| 12 |
| 24 |
| 37 |
| 50 |
| 62 |
| 76 |
| 90 |
| 103 |
| 114 |

In the last lesson, you read about the cardiovascular system. This organ system is one of several systems that perform specific life functions. Organ systems consist of organs and tissues that work together to perform specific jobs. However, organs such as the heart, liver, kidneys, or lungs can become diseased and unable to perform their job efficiently, leading to life-threatening illnesses. When a person's life is threatened because of a weakened or damaged organ, an organ transplant can be performed. In this article, you will read about one type of organ transplant, the **heart transplant**, the first of which was completed in December 1967. At that time, it was an extremely experimental procedure. Today, however, heart transplants save thousands of lives each year. (#1)

| 124 |
| 131 |
| 145 |
| 157 |
| 171 |
| 183 |
| 196 |
| 210 |
| 220 |
| 231 |

Who Is Eligible for a New Heart?

Heart disease is one of the leading causes of death among both men and women. Doctors prescribe many types of medicines to people who have heart disease; however, when a person's heart is failing in spite of all other therapies, that person may become a candidate for a heart transplant. Generally, the patients should be under 60 and in good health other than having advanced heart disease. People who have other health problems may not be eligible for a transplant. Because their immune system is weakened during the transplant procedure, people with an already weak immune system or other health problems would be too susceptible to, or too likely to get, an infection. (#2)

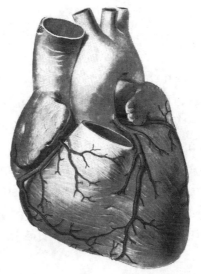

B

244	**What Must Happen Before the Transplant?**
250	Once a patient is accepted for a transplant, their name goes on a waiting list.
265	They must wait until a suitable donor heart is located. Donor hearts usually
278	come from people who are brain dead. This means that their brains no longer
292	function, but their bodies do. Their organs, including their heart, are still
304	healthy. **Donors** are people who have specified to their family and friends that
317	they are willing to donate organs when they die. Doctors must have this
330	permission in order to use donor organs for transplants. (#3)
339	People on the waiting list must wait until a heart becomes available that
352	matches their blood and tissue type. Except when organs are donated from an
365	identical twin, donor organs will be somewhat incompatible with those of the
377	recipient. Nevertheless, it is important to find a heart that is as similar to the
392	recipient's blood and tissue type as possible.
399	Unfortunately, the waiting list is a major barrier to people receiving needed
411	transplants. The list is long, and not enough donor organs are available. The
424	medical community is trying to educate people about how important it is to
437	designate themselves as organ donors before they die so that more people will
450	choose to be organ donors. (#4)

C

455	**What Occurs During the Surgery?**
460	When a suitable donor is found, the donor heart is removed from the body
474	and packed in special chemicals that will help to preserve the heart while in
488	transport. It is then packed in a cooler of ice and quickly brought to the hospital
504	where the transplant patient is prepared for surgery. As soon as the new heart
518	arrives, the surgery begins. (#5)
522	The surgery takes about five hours. First, doctors put the patient to sleep
535	with an anesthetic. Next, they open the patient's chest and remove the diseased
548	heart. Meanwhile, the patient is hooked up to a heart-lung machine. This
561	machine functions as the patient's heart and lungs during surgery, allowing
572	oxygen and blood to continue flowing through the body. It also cools the blood,
586	which protects the other organs. The doctors sew the new heart's blood vessels
599	into the blood vessels in the patient's chest. Once the heart is connected
612	properly, the blood is warmed gradually. The new heart starts to beat. Once the
626	doctors are sure it is working properly, they suture (sew or close up) the patient's
641	chest and bring him or her to the recovery room. Most patients regain
654	consciousness in a few hours, and leave the hospital within a week. (#6)

D

| 666 | **What Is Necessary After the Transplant?**
| 672 | Heart transplant patients generally return to normal lives. It is, however, very
| 684 | important that they incorporate special medications into their routine. These
| 694 | medications ensure that the body accepts the new heart. Normally, the body's
| 706 | immune system gets rid of or rejects foreign material. Doctors need to prevent the
| 720 | body from rejecting the new heart, which the body experiences as foreign material.
| 733 | Special drugs suppress, or restrain, the patient's immune system. Otherwise, the
| 744 | body might see the new heart as foreign and reject it. As long as these drugs are
| 761 | successful, heart transplant patients are able to continue their lives, thanks to the
| 774 | generosity of people who were willing to share their organs. (#7)
| 784 |

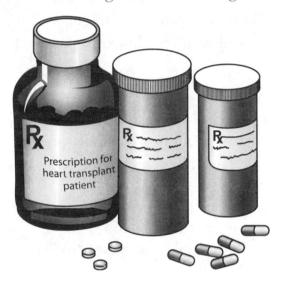

Prescription for
heart transplant
patient

(ACTIVITY D) *Fluency Building*

Cold Timing [ ]   **Practice 1** [ ]

Practice 2 [ ]   **Hot Timing** [ ]

ACTIVITY E *Comprehension Questions—Multiple Choice*

Comprehension Strategy—Multiple Choice

Step 1: Read the item.

Step 2: Read all of the choices.

Step 3: Think about why each choice might be correct or incorrect. Check the article as needed.

Step 4: From the possible correct choices, select the best answer.

1. (Cause and effect) **Which person is most likely to be eligible for a heart transplant?**
   a. Pete—a wealthy 80-year-old with lung cancer and a defective heart.
   b. Harry—a 45-year-old with a defective heart and a poor immune system.
   c. Rita—a 50-year-old former professional tennis player with advanced heart disease.
   d. Martha—a 52-year-old with high blood pressure who has just started a diet and exercise program.

2. (Compare and contrast) **Which of the following would be an unnecessary requirement for a person to be a heart donor?**
   a. The individual must be brain-dead with organs that are still healthy.
   b. The individual must have blood and tissue types that match closely that of the recipient.
   c. Prior to death, the organ donor must have told friends and family members that he or she wished to be an organ donor.
   d. Prior to death, the individual must specify to his or her minister, rabbi, or priest his or her desires.

3. (Vocabulary) **Which of these words is related to the word <u>recipient</u>?**
   a. repent
   b. receive
   c. recent
   d. recipe

4. (Main idea) **What is the main idea of this passage?**
   a. The first heart transplants in 1967 were very experimental.
   b. Many people with heart disease can live normal lives if they have the benefit of a donated heart and surgery.
   c. A heart donor must be brain-dead and still have a healthy heart that closely matches the blood and tissue types of the recipient.
   d. One of the perils of heart transplants is the possibility that the body might reject an incompatible heart.

MULTIPLE CHOICE COMPREHENSION 4

Points

(ACTIVITY F) *Vocabulary Activities*

Yes/No/Why

1. Is **surgery suitable** for most **patients**?

_____

_____

_____

_____

2. If you are **susceptible** to a disease, are you **immune** to it?

_____

_____

_____

_____

3. Is **anesthetic incompatible** with **consciousness**?

_____

_____

_____

_____

Completion Activities

1. **donation:** something you give
Some organizations that accept donations are

_____

_____

_____

_____

2. **permitted:** allowed to
Special events that you are permitted to attend include

_____

_____

_____

_____

3. **gradually:** little by little; slowly
Some things happen very quickly in life, but these things happen gradually:

_____

_____

_____

_____

4. **generosity:** willingness to give or share freely
People demonstrate their generosity by

_____

_____

_____

_____

VOCABULARY | 7

Points

(ACTIVITY G) *Expository Writing—Multi-Paragraph Answer*

Writing Strategy—Multi-Paragraph Answer

Step 1: LIST (List the details that are important enough to include in your answer.)

　　Step 2: CROSS OUT (Reread the details. Cross out any that don't go with the topic.)
　　Step 3: CONNECT (Connect any details that could go into one sentence.)
　　Step 4: NUMBER (Number the details in a logical order.)
　　Step 5: WRITE (Write the paragraph.)
Step 6: EDIT (Revise and proofread your answer.)

Prompt: Describe what occurs during each stage of a heart transplant: before surgery, during surgery, and after surgery.

Plan: Complete the Planning Box with your teacher.

Example Multi-Paragraph Plan

Planning Box
(topic a) *before surgery*
(detail) – *must be eligible*
(detail) – *eligible—under 60 and otherwise healthy*
(detail) – *goes on waiting list*
(detail) – *wait for suitable donor heart*
(detail) – *must match blood and tissue type of recipient*
(topic b) *during surgery*
(detail)
(detail)
(detail)
(detail)
(detail)
(detail)
(detail)
(detail)
(detail)
(topic c) *after surgery*
(detail)
(detail)
(detail)
(detail)

Write: Write paragraphs a, b, and c on a separate piece of paper.

Evaluate: Evaluate the paragraphs using this rubric.

Rubric— Multi-Paragraph Answer	Student or Partner Rating		Teacher Rating	
1. Did the author state the topic in the first sentence?	a. Yes Fix up b. Yes Fix up c. Yes Fix up		a. Yes No b. Yes No c. Yes No	
2. Did the author include details that go with the topic?	a. Yes Fix up b. Yes Fix up c. Yes Fix up		a. Yes No b. Yes No c. Yes No	
3. Did the author combine details in some of the sentences?	a. Yes Fix up b. Yes Fix up c. Yes Fix up		a. Yes No b. Yes No c. Yes No	
4. Is the answer easy to understand?	Yes Fix up		Yes No	
5. Did the author correctly spell words, particularly the words found in the article?	Yes Fix up		Yes No	
6. Did the author use correct capitalization, capitalizing the first word in the sentence and proper names of people, places, and things?	Yes Fix up		Yes No	
7. Did the author use correct punctuation, including a period at the end of each sentence?	Yes Fix up		Yes No	

6

ACTIVITY H *Comprehension—Single-Paragraph Answer*

Writing Strategy—Single-Paragraph Answer

Step 1: Read the item.
Step 2: Turn the question into part of the answer and write it down.
Step 3: Think of the answer or locate the answer in the article.
Step 4: Complete your answer.

Prompt:

What Is—Heart transplants can significantly improve an individual's length and quality of life.

What If—What would your chances be of being on a heart transplant waiting list IF you smoked, did not exercise, and were overweight? Explain your answer.

Write and Discuss: Write a paragraph. Then share your ideas. Use the Discussion Guidelines.

Discussion Guidelines

Speaker		Listener	
Looks like:	**Sounds like:**	**Looks like:**	**Sounds like:**
• Facing peers • Making eye contact • Participating	• Using pleasant, easy-to-hear voice • Sharing opinions, supporting facts and reasons from the article and from your experience • Staying on the topic	• Facing speaker • Making eye contact • Participating	• Waiting quietly to speak • Giving positive, supportive comments • Disagreeing respectfully

WRITING **DISCUSSION**

4 4

Points   Points

(**ACTIVITY A**) *Vocabulary*

List 1: Tell

1. **virus**   *n.*   ▶ (a tiny, infectious particle)
2. **polyhedral**   *adj.* ▶ (having many sides)
3. **genetic**   *adj.* ▶ (related to the development of organisms)
4. **vaccine**   *n.*   ▶ (a dead or weakened virus or bacteria that is used to protect against certain diseases)
5. **antibodies**   *n.*   ▶ (proteins in the blood that destroy germs)

List 2: Strategy Practice

1. **characteristics** *n.*   ▶ (features, qualities, or functions)
2. **replication**   *n.*   ▶ (a close or exact copy)
3. **membrane**   *n.*   ▶ (a thin layer of tissue)
4. **adsorption**   *n.*   ▶ (keeping something on the surface instead of absorbing it)
5. **instructions**   *n.*   ▶ (explanations, directions, or orders)
6. **assembly**   *n.*   ▶ (fitting together parts to make a whole)
7. **administered**   *v.*   ▶ (given to)
8. **bacterial**   *adj.* ▶ (related to bacteria)
9. **information**   *n.*   ▶ (knowledge or facts about things)
10. **significantly**   *adv.* ▶ (a lot)

TALLY ⬚   VOCABULARY **5**

Points

List 3: Word Relatives

	Verb	**Noun**	**Adjective**
Family 1	develop (to grow and change)	development developer	developmental
Family 2	reproduce (to produce others of the same kind)	reproduction	reproducible
Family 3	infect (to cause disease in)	infection	infectious
Family 4	invade (to enter and overrun)	invasion invader	
Family 5	detect (to find out or discover)	detection detective	detectable

(ACTIVITY B) *Spelling Dictation*

1.	4.
2.	5.
3.	6.

ACTIVITY C *Passage Reading and Comprehension*

Note: For this activity, you will need Reproducible G found in the *Teacher's Guide*.

Viruses

A	Have you ever had a cold or the flu? The coughing and sneezing, aches and
15	fevers are all the work of a tiny virus living inside some of your body's cells. How
32	can such a tiny thing cause you to feel so awful?
43	**What Are Viruses?**
46	All living things, like plants and animals, share common behaviors that
57	include growing, developing, reproducing, and responding to surroundings.
65	Things that do not share these behaviors are nonliving things such as air, metal,
79	and sand. Perched between the boundary of living and nonliving things are
91	**viruses**, which are tiny, infectious particles that are considered by some scientists
103	to be living things and by others to be nonliving things. If viruses are floating
118	around in the air or sitting on a kitchen counter, they are inert, having as much
134	life as a rock. However, unlike nonliving things, viruses can live and reproduce.
147	When they attach to a suitable plant, animal, or bacterial cell, referred to as a
162	**host cell**, they infect and take over the cell. To live and to reproduce, they must
178	invade a host cell and use it. (#1)
185	Viruses are not cells even though they have some substances also found in cells.
199	Viruses are particles that are about a thousand times smaller than bacteria. These
212	tiny particles contain genetic instructions that give the virus its characteristics,
223	such as shape and how to reproduce. Viruses are wrapped in a protein coat. Some
238	types of viruses also have a membrane around the protein. (#2)

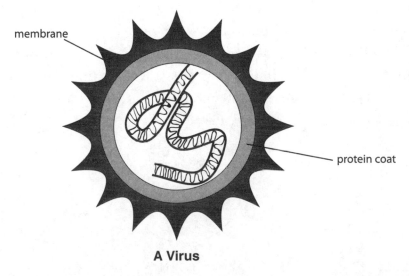

A Virus

B

248	**How Do You Get Infected?**
253	Viruses are around you all the time. They enter your body through your
266	mouth or nose or through breaks in your skin. Different types of viruses require
280	different types of host cells. The protein coat on the virus helps it detect the
295	right kind of host cell. For example, a virus that causes a respiratory infection
309	would detect and attack cells that line the lungs. (#3)
318	Once the host cell is detected, the virus attaches itself to the outside of the
333	cell (*adsorption*). It then injects its genetic information through the cell
344	membrane and into the host cell (*entry*). The host cell's enzymes obey the virus's
358	genetic instructions, creating new virus particles (*replication* and *assembly*).
367	New particles leave the host cell in search of other host cells, where the cycle
382	then continues (*release*). The host cell may be destroyed during this process. As
395	the virus spreads, you begin to feel more and more sick. Carefully examine the
409	flowchart below to better understand how viruses work. (#4)

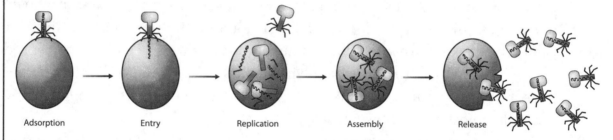

Adsorption   Entry   Replication   Assembly   Release

C

417	**What Do Viruses Look Like?**
422	In order to look at a virus, you would have to look through an electron
437	microscope. Electron microscopes are much more powerful than those you use
448	at school, which may only be able to see bacteria. Remember that viruses are
462	many times smaller than most bacteria cells. Scientists use electron microscopes
473	to see the tiniest of particles.
479	Different kinds of viruses have different shapes. Some viruses are polyhedral,
490	meaning that they have many sides, while some are stick-shaped. Others look
503	like they have pieces of string looped around them. One very common virus is
517	shaped like a spaceship. (#5)

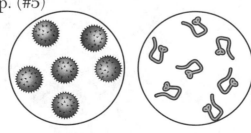

Rotavirus   Ebola Virus

D

521	**How Can We Be Protected From Viruses?**
528	Some basic steps can be taken to reduce the spread of viruses. People who
542	have a cold or the flu should cover their mouths with a tissue when coughing or
558	sneezing to help prevent others from getting the virus. They should also wash
571	their hands before having contact with food or with other people. (#6)
582	In addition, vaccines can be administered against some viruses. While a
593	vaccine cannot cure a virus in someone who already has it, a vaccine can prevent
608	a virus from infecting a person who doesn't have it yet. Vaccines teach the body
623	how to produce proteins, called **antibodies**, which can intercept the virus in the
636	bloodstream. An antibody acts like a key, which fits the keyhole on the virus and
651	locks it up. Some groups of people do not have antibodies against some diseases
665	and other people do. Because they didn't have the matching antibodies, many of
678	the first people who lived in the Americas in the 1600s were killed by viruses
693	carried across the ocean by Europeans. In the current century, many people do
706	have antibodies against the virus that causes AIDS, and thus they don't become
719	ill even though they are infected. Yet, these infected people can still infect other
733	people, some of whom might not have the antibodies. (#7)
742	An entirely new strain of a virus may appear even when a tiny change
756	occurs in its genetic code, or instructions. The virus's genetic code can change
769	rapidly, and it can significantly change the virus's shape. When the shape of the
783	virus changes, the antibody key is no longer able to lock up the new virus.
798	Because of this, vaccines often have to be updated frequently to prevent new
811	waves of infection. (#8)
814	Our ability to see and understand viruses and bacteria has greatly increased
826	in just the last twenty-five years. However, no matter what defenses we create,
840	the genetic codes of viruses and bacteria are easily changed and create new
853	problems for us to try to solve.
860	

(ACTIVITY D) *Fluency Building*

Cold Timing [   ]   **Practice 1** [   ]

Practice 2 [   ]   **Hot Timing** [   ]

(ACTIVITY E) *Comprehension Questions—Multiple Choice*

Comprehension Strategy—Multiple Choice

Step 1: Read the item.

Step 2: Read all of the choices.

Step 3: Think about why each choice might be correct or incorrect. Check the article as needed.

Step 4: From the possible correct choices, select the best answer.

1. (Vocabulary) **In the article, the author says that a virus can be inert, having as much life as a rock. This statement means that a virus:**

   a. can experience erosion.

   b. can have no life at times.

   c. can be shaped like a variety of rocks.

   d. can reproduce and grow at any time.

2. (Compare and contrast) **How are viruses DIFFERENT from living things?**

   a. Living things grow and develop. Viruses do not.

   b. Living things reproduce. Viruses do not.

   c. Living things are never inert. In some cases, viruses are inert.

   d. Living things can change. Viruses do not.

3. (Cause and effect) **In order for a virus to live and produce, it must:**

   a. be invaded by a host cell.

   b. invade the right kind of host cell.

   c. be invaded by the right kind of host cell.

   d. be detected by the right kind of host cell using a protein coat.

4. (Main idea) **Which of the following might be a better title for this article?**

   a. Viruses & Bacteria

   b. Viruses—What They Are and How They Work

   c. Vaccines—A Cure?

   d. Viruses—Secret in the DNA

MULTIPLE CHOICE COMPREHENSION $\boxed{4}$

Points

ACTIVITY F *Vocabulary Activities*

Yes/No/Why

1. Does a **virus** carry **information**?

_____

_____

_____

_____

2. Do **genetic instructions** influence **characteristics**?

_____

_____

_____

_____

3. Is **adsorption** part of **replication**?

_____

_____

_____

_____

Completion Activities

1. **significantly:** a lot
   Your ability to get good grades increases significantly when you

   _____

   _____

   _____

   _____

2. **reproduce:** to produce others of the same kind
   Ways to reproduce music include

   _____

   _____

   _____

   _____

3. **assembly:** fitting together parts to make a whole
   Several things require assembly when you bring them home from the store. Name five of those things.

   _____

   _____

   _____

   _____

4. **developing:** growing and changing
   Some signs that a neighborhood is developing are

   _____

   _____

   _____

   _____

(ACTIVITY G) *Expository Writing—Multi-Paragraph Answer*

Writing Strategy—Multi-Paragraph Answer

Step 1: LIST (List the details that are important enough to include in your answer.)

    Step 2: CROSS OUT (Reread the details. Cross out any that don't go with the topic.)

    Step 3: CONNECT (Connect any details that could go into one sentence.)

    Step 4: NUMBER (Number the details in a logical order.)

    Step 5: WRITE (Write the paragraph.)

Step 6: EDIT (Revise and proofread your answer.)

Prompt: Explain each big idea in this article about viruses: what they are like, how they reproduce, and how we can protect ourselves and others from infection.

Plan: Complete the Planning Box with your teacher.

APPLICATION LESSON

7

Example Multi-Paragraph Plan

Planning Box
(topic a) *viruses—what they are like*
(detail) *– very tiny, infectious particles*
(detail) *– considered by some as living*
(detail) *– can live and reproduce if they invade host cells*
(detail) *– considered by some as nonliving*
(detail) *– in air or on surface, inert*
(detail) *– much smaller than bacteria*
(detail) *– not cells*
(detail) *– contain genetic instructions*
(topic b) *viruses—how they reproduce*
(detail)
(detail)
(detail)
(detail)
(detail)
(detail)
(detail)
(topic c) *viruses—how we can protect ourselves and others from infection*
(detail)
(detail)
(detail)
(detail)
(detail)

Write: Write paragraphs a, b, and c on a separate piece of paper.

Evaluate: Evaluate the paragraphs using this rubric.

Rubric— Multi-Paragraph Answer	Student or Partner Rating		Teacher Rating	
1. Did the author state the topic in the first sentence?	a. Yes Fix up b. Yes Fix up c. Yes Fix up		a. Yes No b. Yes No c. Yes No	
2. Did the author include details that go with the topic?	a. Yes Fix up b. Yes Fix up c. Yes Fix up		a. Yes No b. Yes No c. Yes No	
3. Did the author combine details in some of the sentences?	a. Yes Fix up b. Yes Fix up c. Yes Fix up		a. Yes No b. Yes No c. Yes No	
4. Is the answer easy to understand?	Yes Fix up		Yes No	
5. Did the author correctly spell words, particularly the words found in the article?	Yes Fix up		Yes No	
6. Did the author use correct capitalization, capitalizing the first word in the sentence and proper names of people, places, and things?	Ycs Fix up		Yes No	
7. Did the author use correct punctuation, including a period at the end of each sentence?	Yes Fix up		Yes No	

WRITING **13**
Points

7

(ACTIVITY H) *Comprehension—Single-Paragraph Answer*

Writing Strategy—Single-Paragraph Answer

Step 1: Read the item.
Step 2: Turn the question into part of the answer and write it down.
Step 3: Think of the answer or locate the answer in the article.
Step 4: Complete your answer.

Prompt:

What Is—In order for a virus to reproduce, it must attach itself to a specific type of host cell. Thus, viruses cannot attach to all cells.

What If—What if viruses could attach to any plant or animal cell and reproduce in all situations?

Write and Discuss: Write a paragraph. Then share your ideas. Use the Discussion Guidelines.

Discussion Guidelines

Speaker		Listener	
Looks like:	**Sounds like:**	**Looks like:**	**Sounds like:**
• Facing peers • Making eye contact • Participating	• Using pleasant, easy-to-hear voice • Sharing opinions, supporting facts and reasons from the article and from your experience • Staying on the topic	• Facing speaker • Making eye contact • Participating	• Waiting quietly to speak • Giving positive, supportive comments • Disagreeing respectfully

WRITING   DISCUSSION

Points   Points

(ACTIVITY A) *Vocabulary*

List 1: Tell

1. **Antoni van Leeuwenhoek** *n.* ▶ (the scientist known as the Father of Microbiology)

2. *Micrographia* *n.* ▶ (an influential book introducing the use of the microscope)

3. **Robert Hooke** *n.* ▶ (the author of *Micrographia*)

4. **protozoa** *n.* ▶ (single-celled microscopic animals)

5. **animalcules** *n.* ▶ (old, archaic term for tiny swimming animals)

6. **bacilli** *n.* ▶ (a type of bacteria)

7. **cocci** *n.* ▶ (a type of bacteria)

8. **spirilla** *n.* ▶ (a type of bacteria)

List 2: Strategy Practice

1. **microbiology** *n.* ▶ (the branch of biology that studies microorganisms)

2. **microcosm** *n.* ▶ (the little world of microorganisms)

3. **microscope** *n.* ▶ (an instrument used to see very small things)

4. **microscopy** *n.* ▶ (the process of using a microscope)

5. **specimens** *n.* ▶ (examples)

6. **contemporary** *adj.* ▶ (existing at the same time)

7. **correspondence** *n.* ▶ (exchange of letters)

8. **translated** *v.* ▶ (changed into another language)

9. **financial** *adj.* ▶ (related to money)

10. **security** *n.* ▶ (protection from danger)

TALLY ☐ VOCABULARY 5
Points

List 3: Word Relatives

	Verb	Noun	Adjective
Family 1	assist (to help)	assistance assistant	assistant
Family 2	influence (to change the thought or behavior of)	influence	influential
Family 3	magnify (to cause to look larger)	magnification magnifier	magnifiable
Family 4	adjust (to change or arrange to fit a need)	adjustment	adjustable
Family 5	classify (to arrange in groups according to some system)	classification	classifiable

(ACTIVITY B) *Spelling Dictation*

1.	4.
2.	5.
3.	6.

SPELLING 6
Points

ACTIVITY C Passage Reading and Comprehension

Note: For this activity, you will need Reproducible H found in the *Teacher's Guide*.

Antoni van Leeuwenhoek—The Father of Microbiology

A

13 | Whom do you think of when you think of an important scientist? Someone
28 | who studies science in school for many years and then applies what he or she
40 | learns? Someone who works in a scientific field? Antoni van Leeuwenhoek did
55 | none of these things, but he became one of the best-known scientists in history.
70 | He is often referred to as the Father of Microbiology, the branch of biology that
84 | studies living things that are too small to be seen with the unaided eye.

97 | Van Leeuwenhoek worked in his native country of Holland, first as a fabric
109 | merchant and later as a chamberlain (assistant) to the town's sheriffs. Because
123 | working as a chamberlain gave him a great deal of financial security and free
139 | time, he had time to read many books. In the late 1660s, he was introduced to
150 | microscopes through a book titled *Micrographia* by Robert Hooke. This book
163 | was highly influential and introduced the public to microscopy, the use of the
      | microscope to investigate tiny living things. (#1)

B

169 | **An Unusual Hobby**
172 | This field of study fascinated van Leeuwenhoek. He began to practice
183 | microscopy and developed an unusual hobby. He learned how to grind his own
196 | lenses, and he created his own microscope that differed from the compound
208 | microscopes of that day. Unlike compound microscopes that used more than one
220 | lens, van Leeuwenhoek's microscopes were simple devices that used only one
231 | lens. While the contemporary microscopes of his day magnified a specimen 20 to
244 | 30 times, van Leeuwenhoek's microscopes magnified a specimen 200 to 300
255 | times. This difference was due chiefly to Leeuwenhoek's skill at lens grinding and
268 | his patience in adjusting the light source when viewing tiny specimens. (#2)

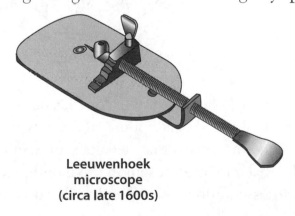

**Leeuwenhoek
microscope
(circa late 1600s)**

C

279	### Van Leeuwenhoek's Observations
282	Once van Leeuwenhoek had developed his powerful, one-lens microscope,
292	his observations expanded and focused on a range of specimens. He observed
304	and described fungi, bee stingers, and lice. He even described creatures that
316	were too small for the human eye to observe unaided. He called these creatures
330	**protozoa**. Protozoa are single-celled microscopic animals. (#3)
337	In 1673, van Leeuwenhoek began a correspondence with the Royal Society
348	of London, a scientific group in England. He sent regular letters that were filled
362	with a jumble of observations about various subjects. Each letter described his
374	experiments and findings. But it wasn't until he described the world he saw in a
389	drop of water that the Royal Society began to take real notice of his work. (#4)

D

404	### An Important Discovery
407	Van Leeuwenhoek discovered that the drop of water was host to many tiny,
420	swimming creatures, which he called **animalcules**. This news caused a great stir
432	in the Royal Society of London. They realized that he must have made an
446	important discovery. He had found a whole new world that is much smaller than
460	anything humans can see with their eyes. The Society set out to reproduce the
474	experiment. Once they had seen the tiny creatures for themselves, they were
486	convinced. This discovery, coupled with van Leeuwenhoek's discovery of
495	protozoa, formed the basis for a new branch of science: **microbiology**. (#5)

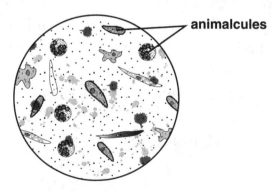

animalcules

drop of water

506	Van Leeuwenhoek did not stop making his observations. He continued his
517	experiments and provided descriptions of many types of bacteria, algae, and
528	other single-celled organisms that scientists are familiar with today. He even
540	discovered that bacteria are present in the mouth. He eventually classified the
552	bacteria he witnessed into three types: bacilli, cocci, and spirilla. He observed

564	plant and muscle tissue. He also discovered red blood cells. Throughout his
576	lifetime, he continued to write to the Royal Society of London, describing his
589	findings and observations. (#6)

E

592	**Recognition**
593	As his letters were translated and published, van Leeuwenhoek became quite
604	famous. He was elected to be part of the Royal Society, though he never actually
619	attended a meeting in London. His discoveries provided a basis for many other
632	types of experiments in the decades to come. Van Leeuwenhoek's exploration of
644	the microcosm set the stage for future advances in technology, medicine, and
656	general research. Our current understandings in microbiology are based upon
666	his work. (#7)
668	Despite his importance to the field of microbiology, he kept his lens-grinding
681	technique a secret. It wasn't until the 19th century, when the compound
693	microscope was improved significantly, that more advances could be made in
704	microbiology. (#8)
705	

(ACTIVITY D) *Fluency Building*

Cold Timing [ ]   **Practice 1** [ ]

Practice 2 [ ]   **Hot Timing** [ ]

(ACTIVITY E) *Comprehension Questions—Multiple Choice*

Comprehension Strategy—Multiple Choice

Step 1: Read the item.

Step 2: Read all of the choices.

Step 3: Think about why each choice might be correct or incorrect. Check the article as needed.

Step 4: From the possible correct choices, select the best answer.

1. (Vocabulary) **You could conclude that "micro" in <u>micro</u>biology means:**
   - **a.** living things.
   - **b.** small.
   - **c.** hot.
   - **d.** microscope.

2. (Cause and effect) **One of the major things that led to Antoni Van Leeuwenhoek's success was:**
   - **a.** the level of education that he received through the Royal Society of London.
   - **b.** his background working as an assistant to the town's sheriff.
   - **c.** his skill at developing powerful microscopes.
   - **d.** his election to the Royal Society of London so he could attend meetings and enhance his scientific knowledge.

3. (Compare and contrast) **When comparing Van Leeuwenhoek's microscopes to compound microscopes of that day, which of the following is NOT a correct statement?**
   - **a.** Van Leeuwenhoek's microscope had one lens while compound microscopes had more than one lens.
   - **b.** Van Leeuwenhoek's microscope magnified a 200 to 300 times while compound microscopes magnified 20 to 30 times.
   - **c.** Van Leeuwenhoek's microscope was simple while compound microscopes were more complex.
   - **d.** Van Leeuwenhoek's microscope was designed to observe small specimens while compound microscopes were designed to examine large items.

4. (Cause and effect) **When Van Leeuwenhoek discovered "tiny swimming creatures" in a drop of water, which of the following did NOT result?**
   - **a.** A new branch of science was formed.
   - **b.** The Royal Society of London knew an important discovery had been made.
   - **c.** He shared his lens-grinding techniques so that other scientists could verify his results.
   - **d.** Van Leeuwenhoek continued his experiments and described many small specimens.

MULTIPLE CHOICE COMPREHENSION 4

(ACTIVITY F) *Vocabulary Activities*

Yes/No/Why

1. Would **microbiology** include the study of **microcosms**?

_____

_____

_____

_____

2. Would you require a **microscope** to study **bacilli specimens**?

_____

_____

_____

_____

3. Could *Micrographia* have provided **Robert Hooke** with **financial security**?

_____

_____

_____

_____

Completion Activities

1. influence: to change the thought or behavior of
Some things in life we have little influence over, but these things we can greatly influence:

_____

_____

_____

_____

2. assistant: one who helps
Although some jobs can be completed by one person, assistants are required for these jobs:

_____

_____

_____

_____

3. correspondence: exchange of letters
In the past, correspondence was difficult because the process was slow.
Correspondence is easier now because

_____

_____

_____

_____

4. translated: changed into another language
In order to be read by people in Spain, France, and Italy, books written in English need to be translated into

_____

_____

_____

_____

VOCABULARY 7

Points

(ACTIVITY G) Expository Writing—Multi-Paragraph Answer

Writing Strategy—Multi-Paragraph Answer

Step 1: LIST (List the details that are important enough to include in your answer.)

Step 2: CROSS OUT (Reread the details. Cross out any that don't go with the topic.)

Step 3: CONNECT (Connect any details that could go into one sentence.)

Step 4: NUMBER (Number the details in a logical order.)

Step 5: WRITE (Write the paragraph.)

Step 6: EDIT (Revise and proofread your answer.)

Prompt: Summarize the information presented on van Leeuwenhoek's hobby, his discoveries, and the recognition of his contributions to science.

Plan: Complete the Planning Box with your teacher.

Example Multi-Paragraph Plan

Planning Box
(topic a) *van Leeuwenhoek—hobby*
(detail) – *read Micrographia*
(detail) – *became interested in the study of small things using microscopes*
(detail) – *created his own microscope*
(detail) – *much more powerful than microscopes of the time*
(detail) – *observed many small things such as fungi, bee stingers, & lice*
(topic b) *van Leeuwenhoek's discoveries*
(detail)
(detail)
(detail)
(detail)
(detail)
(topic c) *van Leeuwenhoek—recognition of scientific contributions*
(detail)
(detail)
(detail)
(detail)
(detail)
(detail)
(detail)

Write: Write paragraphs a, b, and c on a separate piece of paper.

Evaluate: Evaluate the paragraphs using this rubric.

Rubric— Multi-Paragraph Answer	Student or Partner Rating	Teacher Rating
1. Did the author state the topic in the first sentence?	a. Yes Fix up b. Yes Fix up c. Yes Fix up	a. Yes No b. Yes No c. Yes No
2. Did the author include details that go with the topic?	a. Yes Fix up b. Yes Fix up c. Yes Fix up	a. Yes No b. Yes No c. Yes No
3. Did the author combine details in some of the sentences?	a. Yes Fix up b. Yes Fix up c. Yes Fix up	a. Yes No b. Yes No c. Yes No
4. Is the answer easy to understand?	Yes Fix up	Yes No
5. Did the author correctly spell words, particularly the words found in the article?	Yes Fix up	Yes No
6. Did the author use correct capitalization, capitalizing the first word in the sentence and proper names of people, places, and things?	Yes Fix up	Yes No
7. Did the author use correct punctuation, including a period at the end of each sentence?	Yes Fix up	Yes No

(ACTIVITY H) *Comprehension—Single-Paragraph Answer*

Writing Strategy—Single-Paragraph Answer

Step 1: Read the item.
Step 2: Turn the question into part of the answer and write it down.
Step 3: Think of the answer or locate the answer in the article.
Step 4: Complete your answer.

Prompt:

What Is—Because the Royal Society of London recognized the importance of van Leeuwenhoek's discoveries, they repeated and expanded on many of his studies and distributed his findings.

What If—If the Royal Society of London had not recognized the importance of van Leeuwenhoek's discoveries, what might have resulted?

Write and Discuss: Write a paragraph. Then share your ideas. Use the Discussion Guidelines.

Discussion Guidelines

Speaker		Listener	
Looks like:	**Sounds like:**	**Looks like:**	**Sounds like:**
• Facing peers • Making eye contact • Participating	• Using pleasant, easy-to-hear voice • Sharing opinions, supporting facts and reasons from the article and from your experience • Staying on the topic	• Facing speaker • Making eye contact • Participating	• Waiting quietly to speak • Giving positive, supportive comments • Disagreeing respectfully

WRITING DISCUSSION
4 Points   4 Points

ACTIVITY A *Vocabulary*

List 1: Tell

1. **Democritus** *n.* ▶ (the first person to determine that all things must be made up of smaller parts called atoms)

2. **John Dalton** *n.* ▶ (the scientist who proposed modern atomic theory)

3. **nucleus** *n.* ▶ (the center of an atom, containing neutrons and protons)

4. **neutrons** *n.* ▶ (particles with no electrical charge)

5. **protons** *n.* ▶ (positively charged particles)

6. **electrons** *n.* ▶ (negatively charged particles)

List 2: Strategy Practice

1. **compound** *n.* ▶ (a combination of two or more elements)

2. **hydrogen** *n.* ▶ (a colorless, odorless, tasteless gas)

3. **particles** *n.* ▶ (very small bits)

4. **atomic** *adj.* ▶ (related to an atom)

5. **subatomic** *adj.* ▶ (smaller than an atom)

6. **electrical** *adj.* ▶ (having to do with electricity)

7. **negatively** *adv.* ▶ (not positive)

8. **individually** *adv.* ▶ (separately)

9. **attention** *n.* ▶ (focus; thought)

10. **ultimately** *adv.* ▶ (finally)

List 3: Word Relatives

	Verb	Noun	Adjective
Family 1	determine (to give direction to; to find out by observation)	determination determiner	determined
Family 2	discover (to obtain knowledge of for the first time)	discovery discoverer	
Family 3	wonder (to want to know or learn)	wonder	wonderful
Family 4	define (to describe or to state the meaning of)	definition definer	definable
Family 5	suggest (to bring or call to mind)	suggestion	suggestible suggestive

(ACTIVITY B) *Spelling*

1.		**4.**	
2.		**5.**	
3.		**6.**	

SPELLING **6**
Points

(ACTIVITY C) *Passage Reading and Comprehension*

Note: For this activity, you will need Reproducible I found in the *Teacher's Guide.*

Atoms

A

14	Your table may be made of wood. Your toothbrush may be made of plastic. Have you ever stopped to wonder what the plastic and wood are made of? They
29	
42	are made up of elements, like carbon and hydrogen, all arranged in specific ways. But what are these elements made of? If you break down an element into
57	the smallest part of itself that still behaves like that element, you have an atom.
72	An **atom** is the smallest particle of an element that can exist alone. Atoms are
87	the building blocks of all matter. (#1)

B

93	**History**
94	The first person to define an atom was Democritus in 530 B.C. He
107	determined that all things must be made up of smaller parts, and that ultimately
121	they could be broken down into atoms, or that which cannot be divided. His
135	theory suggested that these atoms would make up all substances, even though
147	they were too small to see individually. (#2)
154	In 1808, John Dalton added to the work of Democritus. Dalton stated the
167	following principles:
169	• Every element is made of atoms.
175	• All atoms of any element are the same.
183	• Atoms of different elements are different.
189	• Atoms of different elements can combine to form compounds.
198	• In any compound, the numbers and kinds of atoms remain the same.
210	These principles formed modern atomic theory until the discovery of the
221	electron in 1897. (#3)

C

224	**Simple Atomic Structure**
227	Each atom contains a nucleus at its center. The **nucleus** is a tightly packed
241	cluster of protons (which carry a positive electrical charge) and neutrons (which
253	carry no electrical charge). The protons determine how an atom behaves. Each
265	type of element is defined by the number of protons it contains. This is called
280	the element's **atomic number**. The higher the atomic number, the more the
292	atom weighs. (#4)
294	There is more to an atom than its center. A series of smaller, negatively
308	charged particles, called **electrons**, orbit the nucleus. The electrons are

318
331
341
353
369

significantly smaller, about 1/1860ᵗʰ the size of a proton. If the number of electrons (negatively charged particles) equals the number of protons (positively charged particles), then the atom is electrically neutral. However, if the numbers are not the same, because of a collision or other event, then the atom is called an **ion**. Ions have an electrical charge, either positive or negative. (#5)

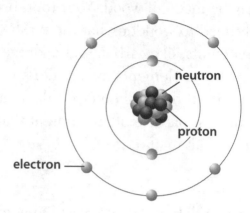

An Oxygen Atom

380
393
409
421
437
449
462

The electrons move very fast and create clouds of energy. These clouds may look much the same as when you wave a sparkler around very fast in the dark. These energy clouds are actually force fields that make specific shapes. The larger an atom is, the more electrons and force fields it has, giving that atom a more complex shape. Atoms are hooked to one another with these electron clouds to form **molecules**. When atoms combine, it's like twisting a bunch of balloons together, creating some really cool, 3D molecules.

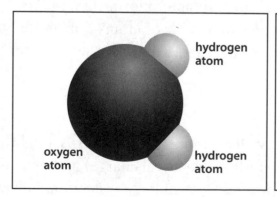
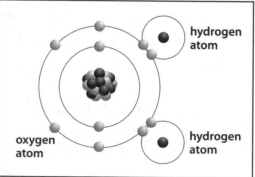

Two Models of a Water Molecule (H₂O)

470
485
498

Consider this: Because the outside of an atom is just an energy field and not solid, you aren't really touching this page; your energy fields are bumping into the energy fields of the paper. (#6)

D

504	**How Do We Know Atoms Exist?**
510	We cannot see atoms with our eyes. We cannot even see them with regular
524	light microscopes, as you might see in a science lab. However, in the early 1980s,
539	a special type of microscope, called a **Scanning Tunneling Microscope** (STM), was
551	invented. It reads a surface by scanning it with tiny electrical currents. These
564	currents interact with the electrical charges of the atoms on the surface. The
577	STM can then generate a sort of atomic map of the surface it is looking at,
593	creating a picture of the atoms and their relationships to one another. (#7)

E

605	**Is There Anything Smaller Than Atoms?**
611	Scientists have now turned their attention to subatomic particles—particles
621	that are smaller than atoms. They are studying the nuclei of atoms more closely,
635	trying to discover even smaller building blocks. They have discovered that many
647	smaller pieces exist. One interesting, small piece is known as the **quark**.
659	Physicists are attempting to construct theories about how quarks interact with
670	one another and how they behave. Many scientists feel that if they can
683	understand the tiny particles that make up everything, they will be able to
696	understand how everything in the universe works. Only time will tell what they
709	find out. (#8)
711	

(ACTIVITY D) *Fluency Building*

Cold Timing [   ]   **Practice 1** [   ]

Practice 2 [   ]   **Hot Timing** [   ]

(ACTIVITY E) *Comprehension Questions—Multiple Choice*

Comprehension Strategy—Multiple Choice

Step 1: Read the item.

Step 2: Read all of the choices.

Step 3: Think about why each choice might be correct or incorrect. Check the article as needed.

Step 4: From the possible correct choices, select the best answer.

1. (Vocabulary) **If you were defining an atom, which of the following would you NOT include as a definition?**

    a. Smallest part of an element that can exist alone.

    b. Smallest part of an element that acts like the element.

    c. Building blocks of all matter.

    d. Smallest element in a substance.

2. (Main idea) **What was the major accomplishment of John Dalton?**

    a. He was the first person to define an atom and explain that all things are made up of atoms.

    b. He stated principles that formed modern atomic theory for almost 100 years.

    c. He was the first scientist to suggest that a substance contained smaller substances.

    d. He determined that all things could be broken down into atoms.

3. (Compare and contrast) **Which of the following comparisons is <u>true</u>?**

    a. Protons carry a positive electrical charge while electrons have a neutral charge.

    b. Protons and electrons are found in the nucleus of an atom.

    c. Protons are found in the nucleus of the atom while electrons orbit the nucleus.

    d. Protons carry a positive electrical charge while neutrons have an opposing negative charge.

4. (Main idea) **The author suggests that "you aren't really touching this page" because:**

    a. the outside of an atom is just an energy field.

    b. all life is an illusion.

    c. an atom cannot be seen by the naked eye.

    d. we cannot detect the protons and electrons.

MULTIPLE CHOICE COMPREHENSION

4

ACTIVITY F *Vocabulary Activities*

Yes/No/Why

1. Can **subatomic particles** be viewed **individually**?

_____

_____

_____

_____

2. Would **protons**, **electrons**, and **neutrons** be found in the **nucleus**?

_____

_____

_____

_____

3. Does **John Dalton's atomic** theory still receive **attention**?

_____

_____

_____

_____

Completion Activities

1. individually: separately
If I were working in a department store, I would wrap these things individually:

_____

_____

_____

_____

2. determine: to give direction to; to find out by observation
If I were a scientist, I would want to determine

_____

_____

_____

_____

3. ultimately: finally
Ultimately in life we all have to decide these three things:

_____

_____

_____

_____

4. attention: focus; thought
I must give my full attention in these situations:

_____

_____

_____

_____

VOCABULARY **7**

Points

(ACTIVITY G) *Expository Writing—Multi-Paragraph Answer*

Writing Strategy—Multi-Paragraph Answer

Step 1: LIST (List the details that are important enough to include in your answer.)

    Step 2: CROSS OUT (Reread the details. Cross out any that don't go with the topic.)

    Step 3: CONNECT (Connect any details that could go into one sentence.)

    Step 4: NUMBER (Number the details in a logical order.)

    Step 5: WRITE (Write the paragraph.)

Step 6: EDIT (Revise and proofread your answer.)

Prompt: Explain and provide information on the following statements: (1) All matter is made of atoms. (2) All atoms have a nucleus. (3) Electrons orbit the nucleus.

Plan: Complete the Planning Box.

Example Multi-Paragraph Plan

Planning Box
(topic a) *All matter is made of atoms.*
(detail)
(detail)
(detail)
(topic b) *All atoms have a nucleus.*
(detail)
(detail)
(detail)
(detail)
(topic c) *Electrons orbit the nucleus.*
(detail)
(detail)
(detail)
(detail)

Write: Write paragraphs a, b, and c on a separate piece of paper.

Evaluate: Evaluate the paragraphs using this rubric.

Rubric— Multi-Paragraph Answer	Student or Partner Rating		Teacher Rating	
1. Did the author state the topic in the first sentence?	a. Yes Fix up b. Yes Fix up c. Yes Fix up		a. Yes No b. Yes No c. Yes No	
2. Did the author include details that go with the topic?	a. Yes Fix up b. Yes Fix up c. Yes Fix up		a. Yes No b. Yes No c. Yes No	
3. Did the author combine details in some of the sentences?	a. Yes Fix up b. Yes Fix up c. Yes Fix up		a. Yes No b. Yes No c. Yes No	
4. Is the answer easy to understand?	Yes Fix up		Yes No	
5. Did the author correctly spell words, particularly the words found in the article?	Yes Fix up		Yes No	
6. Did the author use correct capitalization, capitalizing the first word in the sentence and proper names of people, places, and things?	Yes Fix up		Yes No	
7. Did the author use correct punctuation, including a period at the end of each sentence?	Yes Fix up		Yes No	

WRITING | 13
Points

(ACTIVITY H) *Comprehension—Single-Paragraph Answer*

Writing Strategy—Single-Paragraph Answer

Step 1: Read the item.
Step 2: Turn the question into part of the answer and write it down.
Step 3: Think of the answer or locate the answer in the article.
Step 4: Complete your answer.

Prompt:

What Is—A special type of microscope, the Scanning Tunneling Microscope, allows us to create a picture of atoms and their relationships to one another.

What If—What would have happened if we had never developed the Scanning Tunneling Microscope?

Write and Discuss: Write a paragraph. Then share your ideas. Use the Discussion Guidelines.

Discussion Guidelines

Speaker		Listener	
Looks like:	**Sounds like:**	**Looks like:**	**Sounds like:**
• Facing peers • Making eye contact • Participating	• Using pleasant, easy-to-hear voice • Sharing opinions, supporting facts and reasons from the article and from your experience • Staying on the topic	• Facing speaker • Making eye contact • Participating	• Waiting quietly to speak • Giving positive, supportive comments • Disagreeing respectfully

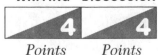

WRITING   DISCUSSION

4   4

Points   Points

(ACTIVITY A) *Vocabulary*

List 1: Tell

1. **Rachel Carson**   *n.* ▶ (a famous naturalist who studied nature)
2. **biology**   *n.* ▶ (the science of living organisms)
3. **zoology**   *n.* ▶ (a branch of biology that focuses on animals)
4. **articles**   *n.* ▶ (writings on a subject)
5. **rebuttals**   *n.* ▶ (opposing arguments)

List 2: Strategy

1. **naturalist**   *n.* ▶ (a person who studies nature)
2. **enamored**   *v.* ▶ (really liked)
3. **concentrate**   *v.* ▶ (to focus on)
4. **pesticide**   *n.* ▶ (a chemical used to destroy plants or animals)
5. **extremely**   *adv.* ▶ (very great)
6. **infestations**   *n.* ▶ (growth in large numbers)
7. **legislative**   *adj.* ▶ (legal)
8. **department**   *n.* ▶ (a section or division of a larger organization, such as a government, a company, or a school)
9. **irrevocably**   *adv.* ▶ (unchangeable)
10. **materials**   *n.* ▶ (things needed to do something)

List 3: Word Relatives

	Verb	Noun	Adjective
Family 1	conserve (to protect from loss, harm, or waste)	conservation conservationist	conservative
Family 2	realize (to understand completely)	realization	realistic
Family 3	produce (to make)	production producer	productive
Family 4	publish (to produce and sell a book or other written material)	publication publisher	publishable
Family 5	represent (to speak for)	representation representative	representative

(ACTIVITY B) *Spelling Dictation*

1.	4.
2.	5.
3.	6.

SPELLING 6
Points

ACTIVITY C *Passage Reading and Comprehension*

Note: For this activity, you will need Reproducible J found in the *Teacher's Guide.*

Rachel Carson, Famous Naturalist

A

10

25

38

50

Born in 1907 in Springdale, Pennsylvania, Rachel Carson was always enamored with nature. As a child, she played by the river that ran through her hometown. When she got older, she studied biology and zoology, a branch of biology that focuses on animals, at the Pennsylvania College for Women and Johns Hopkins University. (#1)

B

53

64

77

88

99

112

128

144

158

174

Following five years of teaching zoology at the University of Maryland, Rachel Carson worked for the next seventeen years with the Fish and Wildlife Service, an agency of the United States' government. There, she wrote conservation materials and scientific articles based on her research. She also wrote books concerning studies of nature. In 1951, she published a book she had written as a study of the ocean called *The Sea Around Us*, which became a bestseller in the fall of 1952. She followed this in 1955 with a book called *The Edge of the Sea*. These books made her a famous naturalist. She became known as a science writer for the public. In 1952, she left the Fish and Wildlife Service to write full time. (#2)

C

178

180

192

Her Beliefs

All of Carson's writings shared a similar theme. She believed that human beings were part of nature, not in charge of it. The difference between other

206	creatures and ourselves is that we have the power to change nature at will,
220	sometimes irrevocably, allowing no return to nature's original state. However,
230	Carson believed that human beings should not use their power to enact drastic
243	change on their environment. She realized that this is exactly what was
255	occurring, and she set out to write the truth. (#3)

D

264	**Concerns About DDT**
267	At the time, DDT was an extremely popular, widely used chemical pesticide
279	designed to kill insects. People considered it a "miracle" substance, capable of
291	controlling many insect infestations. Between 1946 and 1955, the production of
302	DDT increased by nearly 500 million pounds. The chemical industry, the
313	government, and the Public Health Department endorsed its use. (#4)

322	However, not everyone believed DDT was amazing stuff. As early as 1946,
334	naturalists and scientists wrote about the dangers of DDT to fish, mammals, and
347	birds. They described how DDT-laden earthworms were poisoning robins. They
358	observed that mammals and fish had significant levels of DDT in their fatty
371	tissues. Even the U.S. Congress kept track of the numbers of fish killed by
385	DDT. Yet, the public did not hear about these effects of their miracle substance.
399	They only knew that DDT was easy to use and produced quick benefits. (#5)
412	Rachel Carson was familiar with the early studies of the effects of DDT from
426	her work with the Fish and Wildlife Service. She had proposed an article on the
441	dangers of the pesticide to *Reader's Digest*, but they turned it down. Carson
454	already knew she wanted to write another book about humans and ecology, so she
468	decided to concentrate on the damage done to the environment by pesticides.

480
495 The book would be called *Silent Spring*, because of the death of the birds that were ingesting (eating) the DDT, making their songs absent in springtime. (#6)

Effects of DDT

E

506 **Controversy Over Her Book**

510
522
535
545
558
568
579 Even before the book was published, *Silent Spring* caused an uproar. The chemical industry could lose a lot of money if people stopped buying their products in large quantities. Representatives of the industry attacked Rachel Carson and her research through articles, press releases, and letters. But all of the rebuttals (opposing arguments) generated by the chemical industry only caused the book to have more publicity. President Kennedy ordered further research into the effects of pesticides. (#7)

F

585 **Rachel Carson's Legacy**

588
602
615
629
641
652
665
678
688 Because of the attention that *Silent Spring* brought to the use of pesticides in America, many legislative bills were introduced to regulate the use of pesticides. In 1972, DDT was banned. Since that time, some of the wildlife threatened by the chemical has made progress towards recovery, although the pesticide is still present in the environment. In the United States, the Environmental Protection Agency (EPA) was formed in response to heightened awareness of human effects on the environment. People are more aware of the effects pesticides might have on life. Many are choosing pesticide-free farming, gardening, and organic produce. (#8)

(ACTIVITY D) *Fluency Building*

Cold Timing [ ]   **Practice 1** [ ]

Practice 2 [ ]   **Hot Timing** [ ]

(**ACTIVITY E**) *Comprehension Questions—Multiple Choice*

Comprehension Strategy—Multiple Choice

Step 1: Read the item.
Step 2: Read all of the choices.
Step 3: Think about why each choice might be correct or incorrect. Check the article as needed.
Step 4: From the possible correct choices, select the best answer.

1. (Vocabulary) **When the author states that Rachel Carson was "enamored with nature," she means:**
   a. Rachel wanted to armor herself against the dangers of nature.
   b. Rachel wanted to get her teeth's enamel into nature.
   c. Rachel was fascinated by nature.
   d. Rachel knew since childhood that she wanted to study nature.

2. (Main idea) **Which of the following statements would best summarize Rachel Carson's primary beliefs?**
   a. All creatures, including humans, are part of nature, and humans should proceed with care in changing the environment.
   b. All creatures, including humans, are part of nature, but humans have the ability to control nature and should use that power.
   c. All creatures are part of nature and experience growth, development, and reproduction.
   d. All creatures are part of nature and thus affected by the environment.

3. (Vocabulary) **Rachel Carson titled her book *Silent Spring* because:**
   a. she often wrote by a river spring that ran through her hometown.
   b. animals such as frogs and fish that would normally be found in a spring would be killed by DDT, making the spring silent.
   c. birds that ate things sprayed with DDT often died and, as a result, in the spring their songs were no longer heard.
   d. by the spring of 1951, Rachel Carson no longer wanted to be silent about DDT.

4. (Cause and effect) **Who probably disagreed the most with the ideas presented in *Silent Spring*?**
   a. Industrial leaders in the publishing field.
   b. President Kennedy's environmental advisors.
   c. Republicans opposing President Kennedy.
   d. Industrial leaders in the chemical field.

MULTIPLE CHOICE COMPREHENSION

ACTIVITY F Vocabulary Activities

Yes/No/Why

1. Would a **naturalist** generally be **enamored** with **legislative** issues?

_____

_____

_____

_____

2. Could insect **infestations** be reduced by use of **pesticides?**

_____

_____

_____

_____

3. Could **articles** present **rebuttals?**

_____

_____

_____

_____

Completion Activities

1. realize: to understand completely
Recently, I came to realize that

_____

_____

_____

_____

2. enamored: really liked
When I was in fourth grade, I was enamored with

_____

_____

_____

_____

3. produce: to make
These are some of the things that I can produce:

_____

_____

_____

_____

4. materials: things needed to do something
To produce a birthday card for a friend, I would need the following materials:

_____

_____

_____

_____

VOCABULARY 7
Points

(ACTIVITY G) *Expository Writing—Multi-Paragraph Answer*

Writing Strategy—Multi-Paragraph Answer

Step 1: LIST (List the details that are important enough to include in your answer.)

Step 2: CROSS OUT (Reread the details. Cross out any that don't go with the topic.)

Step 3: CONNECT (Connect any details that could go into one sentence.)

Step 4: NUMBER (Number the details in a logical order.)

Step 5: WRITE (Write the paragraph.)

Step 6: EDIT (Revise and proofread your answer.)

Prompt: Rachel Carson was a fascinating person. Describe her professional life, her beliefs and environmental concerns, and her legacy (outcomes of her work).

Plan: Complete the Planning Box.

Example Multi-Paragraph Plan

Planning Box
(topic a)
(detail)
(detail)
(detail)
(detail)
(detail)
(detail)
(detail)
(detail)
(topic b)
(detail)
(detail)
(detail)
(detail)
(topic c)
(detail)
(detail)
(detail)
(detail)
(detail)
(detail)

Write: Write paragraphs a, b, and c on a separate piece of paper.

Evaluate: Evaluate the paragraphs using this rubric.

Rubric—Multi-Paragraph Answer	Student or Partner Rating	Teacher Rating
1. Did the author state the topic in the first sentence?	a. Yes Fix up b. Yes Fix up c. Yes Fix up	a. Yes No b. Yes No c. Yes No
2. Did the author include details that go with the topic?	a. Yes Fix up b. Yes Fix up c. Yes Fix up	a. Yes No b. Yes No c. Yes No
3. Did the author combine details in some of the sentences?	a. Yes Fix up b. Yes Fix up c. Yes Fix up	a. Yes No b. Yes No c. Yes No
4. Is the answer easy to understand?	Yes Fix up	Yes No
5. Did the author correctly spell words, particularly the words found in the article?	Yes Fix up	Yes No
6. Did the author use correct capitalization, capitalizing the first word in the sentence and proper names of people, places, and things?	Yes Fix up	Yes No
7. Did the author use correct punctuation, including a period at the end of each sentence?	Yes Fix up	Yes No

WRITING 13 *Points*

ACTIVITY H *Comprehension—Single-Paragraph Answer*

Writing Strategy—Single-Paragraph Answer

Step 1: Read the item.
Step 2: Turn the question into part of the answer and write it down.
Step 3: Think of the answer or locate the answer in the article.
Step 4: Complete your answer.

Prompt:

What Is—When Rachel Carson wrote *Silent Spring*, DDT was widely used as a pesticide.

What If—What if Rachel Carson had not written *Silent Spring*?

Write and Discuss: Write a paragraph. Then share your ideas. Use the Discussion Guidelines.

Discussion Guidelines

Speaker		Listener	
Looks like:	**Sounds like:**	**Looks like:**	**Sounds like:**
• Facing peers • Making eye contact • Participating	• Using pleasant, easy-to-hear voice • Sharing opinions, supporting facts and reasons from the article and from your experience • Staying on the topic	• Facing speaker • Making eye contact • Participating	• Waiting quietly to speak • Giving positive, supportive comments • Disagreeing respectfully

WRITING   DISCUSSION

4   4

Points   Points

ACTIVITY A *Vocabulary*

List 1: Tell

1.	fissures	*n.* ▶	(long, narrow openings)
2.	volcanoes	*n.* ▶	(openings in the earth through which molten rock, gases, and rocks are forced out)
3.	lava	*n.* ▶	(the molten, liquid rock that flows up and out of a volcano)
4.	crystallize	*v.* ▶	(to form crystals)
5.	Galapagos Islands	*n.* ▶	(islands in the eastern Pacific Ocean)
6.	enzymes	*n.* ▶	(chemical substances produced in the cells of all plants and animals)
7.	archaea*	*n.* ▶	(a type of microorganism)

List 2: Strategy Practice

1.	volcanic	*adj.* ▶	(related to a volcano)
2.	submarine	*n.* ▶	(a ship that can go underwater)
3.	hydrothermal	*adj.* ▶	(having to do with the action of hot liquids or gases)
4.	abnormal	*adj.* ▶	(very different from normal)
5.	temperatures	*n.* ▶	(degree of heat or coldness)
6.	biological	*adj.* ▶	(related to the study of living things)
7.	incredibly	*adv.* ▶	(hard to believe)
8.	medicinal	*adj.* ▶	(related to medicine)
9.	ordinary	*adj.* ▶	(commonly used)
10.	potentially	*adv.* ▶	(possibly)

* Pronounced ARE-kee-uh; formerly known as *archaebacteria*

TALLY ☐   VOCABULARY **5**

Points   *Student Book: Application Lesson 11*   **135**

List 3: Word Relatives

	Verb	Noun	Adjective
Family 1	solidify (to make solid or hard)	solid	solid-state
Family 2	document (to furnish evidence)	document documentary documentation	documentary
Family 3	react (to respond to something)	reaction reactants reactionary	reactionary reactive
Family 4	surround (to enclose on all sides)	surrounding	surrounding
Family 5	descend (to go down)	descent	descendant

ACTIVITY B *Spelling Dictation*

1.	4.
2.	5.
3.	6.

SPELLING 6

Points

ACTIVITY C *Passage Reading and Comprehension*

Note: For this activity, you will need Reproducible K found in the *Teacher's Guide*.

Deep-Sea Vents

A

What Are Hydrothermal Vents?

4   A mile under the ocean's surface, scientists have discovered a strange, foreign
16 world. They found deep cracks, called **fissures**, in the ocean floor. Some of these
30 fissures are small—only half an inch wide. Some are as large as a football
45 stadium. Some fissures spew very hot, mineral-rich water, so scientists call them
58 **hydrothermal vents**. (#1)

B

60 **How Do Hydrothermal Vents Form?**
65   Just as there are active volcanoes among our land-based mountain ranges,
77 volcanoes are also found underwater. Many of these underwater volcanoes are
88 active, releasing lava and hot water filled with many types of minerals. When
101 this hot water flows onto the ocean floor, some of the minerals solidify and form
116 crystals. They crystallize around the area where the hot water is exiting the rock.
130 Gradually, these crystals form hollow, chimney-like vents through which the hot
142 water flows. Some vents are long and narrow, like tubes, while others are short
156 and wide. (#2)

C

158 **How Do We Know They Are There?**
165   In 1977, a special three-person submarine called **Alvin** made a very deep dive
179 near the Galapagos Islands off the western coast of South America. At those
192 depths, the pressure is great enough to crush ordinary vessels. Alvin is one of only
207 a few submarines in the world that descends deep enough to see things at the
222 bottom of the ocean. The submarine has thick portholes for viewing and has
235 cameras mounted on its outside. While exploring a volcanic ridge at the bottom of
249 the ocean, Alvin's crew discovered a hydrothermal vent. Since then, Alvin's crews
261 have gone on to document numerous deep-sea vents around the world. (#3)

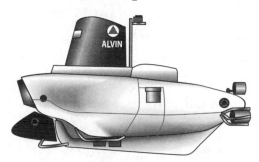

D

273   **Why Is There Economic Interest in Hydrothermal Vents?**

281   Scientists are interested in hydrothermal vents for many reasons. They have

292   discovered that a microorganism called **archaea** thrive in that hot, unfriendly

303   environment. These microorganisms produce enzymes that could potentially be

312   very useful to many of our own industries. These microorganisms might be able

325   to speed up common chemical and biological reactions that are used in

337   industrial processes.

339   Secondly, other forms of life exist in and around these vents. Scientists

351   believe that these life forms might contain compounds that could have

362   medicinal value. Scientists also want to discover how these organisms can exist

374   in such harsh conditions.

378   In addition, the hot water and the vent chimneys contain vast amounts of

391   important metals such as copper, zinc, gold, and iron. People are researching

403   whether it might be possible to mine these resources without harming the

415   hydrothermal vent systems. (#4)

E

418   **What Is Life Like in a Hydrothermal Vent?**

426   Most of the creatures we think of would not be able to survive the incredibly

441   high temperatures surrounding a vent. Because these vents are located in the

453   depths of the ocean, there is no light. Toxic chemicals spew out of the earth. You

469   might think that nothing could live in such an environment. But in reality, many

483   varieties of creatures are suited to live and thrive in these difficult conditions.

496   Archaea are the base of the deep-sea food chain. Instead of using sunlight to

511   photosynthesize like surface-dwelling organisms, these microorganisms collect

519   the energy they need from the minerals coming out of the hydrothermal vents.

532   The archaea use this chemical energy in a process called chemosynthesis to

544   make their food energy and carry out life processes. (#5)

553   Archaea are the prime food source for giant tubeworms and other creatures

565   living near deep-sea vents. Tubeworms that live near hydrothermal vents can

577   grow to be 12 feet tall. Smaller creatures such as eyeless crabs and shrimp crawl

592   around the vents. In such a dark, hostile environment, "abnormal" creatures

603   born with no eyes may actually have a better chance of survival than if they had

619   eyes. These sightless creatures are sensitive to heat and know when they are

632   close to or distant from the vent. In addition, giant clams and other types of

647   mollusks, as well as small fish, sea sponges, and even brittle stars (a type of

662   starfish) live in this hostile, dark place. (#6)

Giant tubeworms and other deep sea creatures live near hydrothermal vents.

669	**Will We Find More Hydrothermal Vents?**
675	Although many vents have been explored in the Pacific and Atlantic Oceans,
687	scientists believe that many more remain undiscovered. Some of these vents
698	may be more than a mile below the surface of the ocean. Scientists continue to
713	learn all that they can about hydrothermal vents and life in the deepest, darkest
727	parts of the earth. One day, they hope that these deep-sea vents may provide
742	vital information about how life first appeared on earth. (#7)
751	

ACTIVITY D *Fluency Building*

Cold Timing [ ]   Practice 1 [ ]

Practice 2 [ ]   Hot Timing [ ]

ACTIVITY E *Comprehension Questions—Multiple Choice*

Comprehension Strategy—Multiple Choice

Step 1: Read the item.
Step 2: Read all of the choices.
Step 3: Think about why each choice might be correct or incorrect. Check the article as needed.
Step 4: From the possible correct choices, select the best answer.

1. (Vocabulary) **The word "hydrothermal" has two meaningful parts. The parts mean:**
   a. hydrogen + sea
   b. hydrogen + thermos
   c. water + mineral
   d. water + hot

2. (Cause and effect) **Which is <u>NOT</u> true of hydrothermal vents?**
   a. Hot, mineral-rich water spews out of hydrothermal vents.
   b. Hydrothermal vents are found on the ocean floor.
   c. Hydrothermal vents are one type of fissure found in the ocean floor.
   d. Hydrothermal vents are found deep within underwater volcanoes.

3. (Cause and effect) **When underwater volcanoes release lava and mineral-rich water:**
   a. some of the minerals become solid and form crystals and gradually form a vent.
   b. the mixtures runs out over the surface of the ocean, creating the base of new volcanoes.
   c. some of the water turns into lava, creating the walls of a volcano.
   d. vent chimneys are formed from the fossil remains of shells and fish.

4. (Cause and effect) **Which statement would be <u>false</u>?**
   a. Most creatures found in the ocean would not be able to survive life in a hydrothermal vent because of the heat.
   b. Most ocean creatures could not survive in the toxic chemicals found at a vent.
   c. Most creatures found in the ocean could not survive without light, which is absent at the vents.
   d. Most ocean creatures would not be able to survive life in or around the hydrothermal vents because of the minerals.

MULTIPLE CHOICE COMPREHENSION

(ACTIVITY F) *Vocabulary Activities*

Yes/No/Why

1. **Potentially**, could a **submarine** explore a **volcano?**

   _____

   _____

   _____

   _____

2. Is it possible to have **abnormal temperatures** at a **hydrothermal** vent?

   _____

   _____

   _____

3. Could something very **ordinary** turn out to be **medicinal?**

   _____

   _____

   _____

   _____

Completion Activities

1. descend: to go down
If I were to descend from the top floor of a building, I might use

_____

_____

_____

_____

2. react: to respond to something
Sometimes we react kindly to others. Other ways that we might react include

_____

_____

_____

_____

3. surrounded: enclosed on all sides
I would hate to be surrounded by water for very long. You would hate to be surrounded by

_____

_____

_____

_____

4. incredibly: hard to believe
An incredibly wonderful meal would include

_____

_____

_____

_____

VOCABULARY 7

Points

ACTIVITY G *Expository Writing—Multi-Paragraph Answer*

Writing Strategy—Multi-Paragraph Answer

Step 1: LIST (List the details that are important enough to include in your answer.)

Step 2: CROSS OUT (Reread the details. Cross out any that don't go with the topic.)

Step 3: CONNECT (Connect any details that could go into one sentence.)

Step 4: NUMBER (Number the details in a logical order.)

Step 5: WRITE (Write the paragraph.)

Step 6: EDIT (Revise and proofread your answer.)

Prompt: Summarize the information on hydrothermal vents using the following topics: (1) What are hydrothermal vents and how are they formed? (2) What is life like in hydrothermal vents? (3) What might be the value in hydrothermal vents?

Plan: Complete the Planning Box.

Example Multi-Paragraph Plan

Planning Box
(topic a)
(detail)
(detail)
(detail)
(detail)
(detail)
(detail)
(detail)
(topic b)
(detail)
(detail)
(detail)
(detail)
(detail)
(detail)
(detail)
(topic c)
(detail)
(detail)
(detail)
(detail)

Write: Write paragraphs a, b, and c on a separate piece of paper.

Evaluate: Evaluate the paragraphs using this rubric.

Rubric— Multi-Paragraph Answer	Student or Partner Rating	Teacher Rating
1. Did the author state the topic in the first sentence?	a. Yes Fix up b. Yes Fix up c. Yes Fix up	a. Yes No b. Yes No c. Yes No
2. Did the author include details that go with the topic?	a. Yes Fix up b. Yes Fix up c. Yes Fix up	a. Yes No b. Yes No c. Yes No
3. Did the author combine details in some of the sentences?	a. Yes Fix up b. Yes Fix up c. Yes Fix up	a. Yes No b. Yes No c. Yes No
4. Is the answer easy to understand?	Yes Fix up	Yes No
5. Did the author correctly spell words, particularly the words found in the article?	Yes Fix up	Yes No
6. Did the author use correct capitalization, capitalizing the first word in the sentence and proper names of people, places, and things?	Yes Fix up	Yes No
7. Did the author use correct punctuation, including a period at the end of each sentence?	Yes Fix up	Yes No

WRITING | 13
Points

11

(ACTIVITY H) *Comprehension—Single-Paragraph Answer*

Writing Strategy—Single-Paragraph Answer

Step 1: Read the item.
Step 2: Turn the question into part of the answer and write it down.
Step 3: Think of the answer or locate the answer in the article.
Step 4: Complete your answer.

Prompt:

What Is—Scientists believe that some of the organisms found in hydrothermal vents may have medicinal value and could be used to cure some diseases.

What If—What would happen if scientists discovered that the strange organisms living in or near deep-sea vents were REALLY valuable to medical research or as a cure to a disease such as cancer?

Write and Discuss: Write a paragraph. Then share your ideas. Use the Discussion Guidelines.

Discussion Guidelines

Speaker		Listener	
Looks like:	**Sounds like:**	**Looks like:**	**Sounds like:**
• Facing peers • Making eye contact • Participating	• Using pleasant, easy-to-hear voice • Sharing opinions, supporting facts and reasons from the article and from your experience • Staying on the topic	• Facing speaker • Making eye contact • Participating	• Waiting quietly to speak • Giving positive, supportive comments • Disagreeing respectfully

WRITING DISCUSSION

4 4
Points Points

(ACTIVITY A) *Vocabulary*

List 1: Tell

1.	earthquakes	*n.* ▶	(vibrations traveling through the earth's crust)
2.	seismologists	*n.* ▶	(scientists who study earthquakes)
3.	seismograph	*n.* ▶	(an instrument used to measure the strength of earthquakes)
4.	aseismic	*adj.* ▶	(related to the absence of earthquakes)
5.	plate tectonics	*n.* ▶	(a theory that says the earth's crust is broken into plates that move)
6.	magnitude	*n.* ▶	(the size of something)
7.	centimeters	*n.* ▶	(small units of measurement)
8.	Richter scale	*n.* ▶	(a scale for representing the strength of earthquakes)
9.	epicenter	*n.* ▶	(the point on the surface of the earth right above the center of the earthquake)

List 2: Strategy Practice

1.	vibration	*n.* ▶	(a rapid movement back and forth)
2.	boundary	*n.* ▶	(a line that marks separation)
3.	instruments	*n.* ▶	(tools for precise and careful work)
4.	satellites	*n.* ▶	(objects that revolve around the earth)
5.	extensive	*adj.* ▶	(large in amount)
6.	eventuality	*n.* ▶	(possibility)
7.	probability	*n.* ▶	(likeliness that something will happen)
8.	protection	*n.* ▶	(keeping from harm)
9.	occurrences	*n.* ▶	(things that happen)
10.	noticeable	*adj.* ▶	(easily noticed)

TALLY ☐ VOCABULARY 5

Points

List 3: Word Relatives

	Verb	Noun	Adjective
Family 1	populate (to supply with people)	population	populous
Family 2	estimate (to make a guess about an amount)	estimation	
Family 3	collide (to crash)	collision	
Family 4	speculate (to think, to ponder)	speculation	speculative
Family 5	prepare (to get ready)	preparation preparedness	preparatory

ACTIVITY B *Spelling Dictation*

1.	4.
2.	5.
3.	6.

SPELLING 6
Points

ACTIVITY C Passage Reading and Comprehension

Note: For this activity, you will need Reproducible L found in the *Teacher's Guide*.

Earthquakes

A

12	Earthquakes occur worldwide on a daily basis even though we only hear about large quakes that occur where people live. It has been estimated that
25	more than three million earthquakes occur yearly with the vast majority being
37	very weak. Stronger earthquakes that have happened in populated areas have
48	caused extensive property damage and loss of life. (#1)

56 **What Is an Earthquake?**

60	To understand earthquakes, first you must understand the structure of the
71	earth. Picture a model of the eath with one section removed so you could see all
87	the layers. At the center of the earth is an **inner core** of solid nickel and iron,
104	surrounded by an **outer core** of molten metals. Around the layer of metals is a
119	layer of rock that is called the earth's **mantle**. The coolest, top-most layer is
134	called the earth's **crust**. When a vibration travels through the earth's crust, it is
148	called an **earthquake**. (#2)

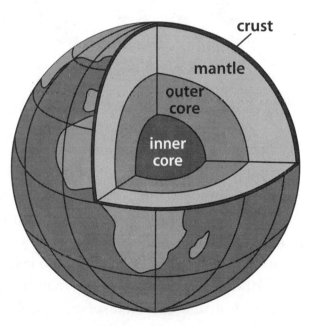

B

151	**What Is the Origin of Earthquakes?**
157	The field of seismology, or the study of earthquakes, changed greatly in the
170	middle of the 20th century when seismologists developed the theory of plate

182	tectonics. According to the plate tectonics theory, the earth's crust is broken
194	into about 7 large and 12 smaller plates, or sections, that slide past or over each
210	other. They drift constantly at very, very slow rates of speed. Plates are like the
225	bumper cars at the fair; plates are in a constant struggle, pulling apart and
239	crashing into each other. Although earthquakes have other causes, the cause of
251	most earthquakes is now attributed to the movement of the earth's plates. (#3)
263	Normally, plates slide past each other at a steady, slow pace of only a few
278	centimeters a year. Scientists call this motion **aseismic creep**. In some instances,
290	however, the friction between the plates is very great, and large sections of rock
304	become stuck against one another. As one section continues moving, the
315	pressure builds until finally the plates become unstuck in one sudden jerk of
328	motion and the force causes a major earthquake to occur. The boundary where
341	two plates met and collided is called a **fault line** or a fault. More earthquakes are
357	highly likely to occur along a fault line. (#4)

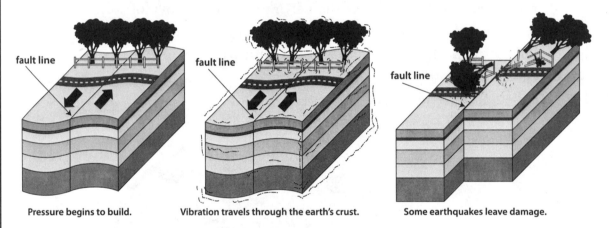

Pressure begins to build.   Vibration travels through the earth's crust.   Some earthquakes leave damage.

C

365	### How Is an Earthquake's Energy Measured?
371	When an earthquake occurs, the force of its vibration creates seismic waves of
384	energy. The release of these seismic waves begins at a point inside the earth called
399	the **focus**. These waves of energy are most felt by humans directly above the focus
414	on the surface at a point called the **epicenter**. The further the energy travels from
429	the epicenter, the weaker it becomes. People who live further away from the
442	epicenter of an earthquake feel less vibration than those who live close by. (#5)
455	Seismologists use instruments called **seismographs** to measure the vibration of
465	the earth during an earthquake. The resulting seismograph readings and the
476	distance from the epicenter are used to determine a rating on a special scale called
491	the **Richter scale**. The ratings on the Richter scale range from 1 to 10. Earthquakes
506	below a 4 aren't very noticeable and do not generally cause much damage. Major
520	earthquakes are rated at 7 and above. The strongest earthquake currently on record

533	measured a 9.5 on the Richter scale. The Richter scale is one common standard for
548	representing the magnitude of earthquakes around the world. (#6)

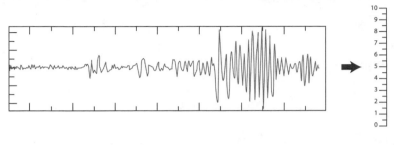

A Seismograph Reading   **Richter Scale**

The seismograph reading and other factors are used to mathematically calculate a
rating on the Richter scale that represents the relative size of an earthquake.

D

556	**How Do We Prepare for "The Big One?"**
564	People who live along fault lines, such as the ones on the western edge of
579	North America, often speculate about "The Big One." Scientists predict that the
591	likelihood of major earthquakes occurring in those regions is increasing. They are
603	able to determine the probability of a major earthquake by using satellites and
616	other advanced equipment to assess how plates are moving. They cannot,
627	however, predict an earthquake. Their instruments allow them to see the patterns
639	that the faults are forming. These patterns can indicate how likely it is that a
654	major earthquake will happen along those faults, but it is impossible to say when.
668	The next major earthquake could occur today or thirty years from now. (#7)
680	To prepare for the eventuality of a major earthquake, people along fault lines
693	learn what to do during an earthquake. Students in schools near fault lines have
707	earthquake drills, just as other students have fire drills. In addition, builders in
720	those areas constantly improve earthquake protection for buildings and large
730	structures. It is important that people in earthquake-prone areas continue to
742	practice earthquake-preparedness. They know that the next big earthquake is
753	coming—they just don't know when. (#8)
759	

(ACTIVITY D) *Fluency Building*

Cold Timing [   ]   **Practice 1** [   ]

Practice 2 [   ]   **Hot Timing** [   ]

12

(ACTIVITY E) *Comprehension Questions—Multiple Choice*

Comprehension Strategy—Multiple Choice

Step 1: Read the item.

Step 2: Read all of the choices.

Step 3: Think about why each choice might be correct or incorrect. Check the article as needed.

Step 4: From the possible correct choices, select the best answer.

1. (Vocabulary) **Which set of words best represents the layers of the earth?**

   a. inner core – outer core — mantle – crust

   b. inner core – crust — outer core — mantle

   c. mantle – crust — inner core — outer core

   d. molten rock — metals — nickel — core

2. (Cause and effect) **According to plate tectonics theory, most earthquakes occur when:**

   a. two large plates slide over each other very slowly.

   b. large sections of rock that have become stuck against one another become unstuck in one sudden jerk.

   c. a plate moves too quickly and collides with another plate.

   d. a volcano erupts and an earthquake soon follows.

3. (Cause and effect) **The force of an earthquake is most likely to be felt by human beings at:**

   a. the focus of the earthquake.

   b. the epicenter.

   c. the earth's core.

   d. a distance of 100 miles from the epicenter.

4. (Compare and contrast) **Which of these would best represent the Richter scale?**

   a.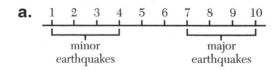

   c.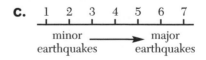

   b.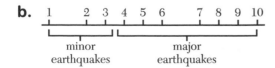

   d.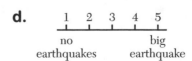

MULTIPLE CHOICE COMPREHENSION 4 *Points*

(**ACTIVITY F**) *Vocabulary*

Yes/No/Why

1. Are **earthquakes** generally represented in **centimeters?**

_____

_____

_____

_____

2. Is there a high **probability** that there will be more **satellites?**

_____

_____

_____

_____

3. Can an **epicenter** be **aseismic?**

_____

_____

_____

_____

Completion Activities

1. speculate: to think, to ponder
When you think of your future, you might speculate about

_____

_____

_____

_____

2. probability: likeliness that something will happen
During the school day, there is a high probability that

_____

_____

_____

_____

3. occurrences: things that happen
Some common occurrences in the morning include

_____

_____

_____

_____

4. prepare: to get ready
To prepare for writing a paper, you might have to

_____

_____

_____

_____

VOCABULARY 7

Points

(ACTIVITY G) *Expository Writing—Multi-Paragraph Answer*

Writing Strategy—Multi-Paragraph Answer

Step 1: LIST (List the details that are important enough to include in your answer.)

　　Step 2: CROSS OUT (Reread the details. Cross out any that don't go with the topic.)

　　Step 3: CONNECT (Connect any details that could go into one sentence.)

　　Step 4: NUMBER (Number the details in a logical order.)

　　Step 5: WRITE (Write the paragraph.)

Step 6: EDIT (Revise and proofread your answer.)

Prompt: Summarize the information provided on the structure of the earth and location of earthquakes; the cause or origin of earthquakes; and the measurement of earthquakes.

Plan: Complete the Planning Box.

Example Multi-Paragraph Plan

Planning Box
(topic a)
(detail)
(detail)
(detail)
(detail)
(topic b)
(detail)
(detail)
(detail)
(detail)
(detail)
(detail)
(topic c)
(detail)
(detail)
(detail)
(detail)

Write: Write paragraphs a, b, and c on a separate piece of paper.

Evaluate: Evaluate the paragraphs using this rubric.

Rubric— Multi-Paragraph Answer	Student or Partner Rating	Teacher Rating
1. Did the author state the topic in the first sentence?	a. Yes Fix up b. Yes Fix up c. Yes Fix up	a. Yes No b. Yes No c. Yes No
2. Did the author include details that go with the topic?	a. Yes Fix up b. Yes Fix up c. Yes Fix up	a. Yes No b. Yes No c. Yes No
3. Did the author combine details in some of the sentences?	a. Yes Fix up b. Yes Fix up c. Yes Fix up	a. Yes No b. Yes No c. Yes No
4. Is the answer easy to understand?	Yes Fix up	Yes No
5. Did the author correctly spell words, particularly the words found in the article?	Yes Fix up	Yes No
6. Did the author use correct capitalization, capitalizing the first word in the sentence and proper names of people, places, and things?	Yes Fix up	Yes No
7. Did the author use correct punctuation, including a period at the end of each sentence?	Yes Fix up	Yes No

WRITING 13 *Points*

(ACTIVITY H) *Comprehension—Single-Paragraph Answer*

Writing Strategy—Single-Paragraph Answer

Step 1: Read the item.
Step 2: Turn the question into part of the answer and write it down.
Step 3: Think of the answer or locate the answer in the article.
Step 4: Complete your answer.

Prompt:

What Is—Earthquakes are highly likely to occur along a fault line where two plates have met and collided.

What if—What if you were living in an earthquake area right on a fault line? What precautions could you take?

Write and Discuss: Write a paragraph. Then share your ideas. Use the Discussion Guidelines.

Discussion Guidelines

Speaker		Listener	
Looks like:	**Sounds like:**	**Looks like:**	**Sounds like:**
• Facing peers • Making eye contact • Participating	• Using pleasant, easy-to-hear voice • Sharing opinions, supporting facts and reasons from the article and from your experience • Staying on the topic	• Facing speaker • Making eye contact • Participating	• Waiting quietly to speak • Giving positive, supportive comments • Disagreeing respectfully

WRITING   DISCUSSION

4	4
Points	Points

(ACTIVITY A) *Vocabulary*

List 1: Tell

1.	meteorologists	*n.* ▶	(people who study the atmosphere and changes within it—especially the weather)
2.	atmosphere	*n.* ▶	(the mass of gases surrounding the earth)
3.	climatologists	*n.* ▶	(people who study climate)
4.	associated	*v.* ▶	(connected in one's mind)
5.	phenomenon	*n.* ▶	(an event that can be observed)
6.	chemistry	*n.* ▶	(the science that deals with how things are made up and how they change when they react with other things)
7.	hurricanes	*n.* ▶	(storms with violent winds)
8.	tornadoes	*n.* ▶	(dark columns of fast-moving air shaped like a funnel)
9.	glaciers	*n.* ▶	(large, slow-moving masses of ice)
10.	supercomputers	*n.* ▶	(very large and fast computers)
11.	typically	*adv.* ▶	(usually)
12.	frequently	*adv.* ▶	(often)

List 2: Strategy Practice

1.	conversation	*n.* ▶	(friendly talk between people)
2.	climatic	*adj.* ▶	(related to typical weather)
3.	conditions	*n.* ▶	(the way things are)
4.	density	*n.* ▶	(thickness)
5.	condensation	*n.* ▶	(the change of a gas to a liquid)
6.	precipitation	*n.* ▶	(any form of water falling to earth)
7.	accompanying	*v.* ▶	(going along with)
8.	alternatively	*adv.* ▶	(on the other hand)
9.	completion	*n.* ▶	(the end; the state of being finished)
10.	productivity	*n.* ▶	(the ability to produce a lot)

TALLY ☐ **VOCABULARY** **5**

Points

List 3: Word Relatives

	Verb	**Noun**	**Adjective**
Family 1	complete (to end; to finish)	completion	complete
Family 2	predict (to declare beforehand)	prediction	predictable
Family 3	direct (to manage or control the course)	direction director	directional
Family 4	create (to cause to exist)	creation creator	creative
Family 5	evaporate (to change a liquid into a gas)	evaporation	evaporable

(ACTIVITY B) *Spelling Dictation*

1.		**4.**	
2.		**5.**	
3.		**6.**	

(ACTIVITY C) *Passage Reading and Comprehension*

Note: For this activity, you will need Reproducible M found in the *Teacher's Guide.*

Weather

A

13 | The weather is frequently a topic of conversation, but few people other than
23 | meteorologists (people who study weather) understand how it happens. Rain,
36 | snow, and even violent storms happen because of the movement of air masses,
50 | the land, the sun's energy, and the jet stream. Before you can understand how
63 | these factors interact to cause weather, you need to understand the rising and
63 | falling of air masses. (#1)

67 | **What Is an Air Mass?**
72 | An **air mass** is a large chunk of air in the earth's atmosphere. It can be
88 | anywhere from ten miles to hundreds or thousands of miles wide, and it can be
103 | warm or cold. Warm and cold air masses are full of moisture. The sun is
118 | constantly causing evaporation of water from the earth's surface and changing
129 | the water (a liquid) into water vapor (a gas consisting of very small drops of
144 | water). The warm air masses contain this water vapor. In cold air masses, the
158 | water vapor has cooled and squeezed together, or condensed, into much larger
170 | drops of water. (#2)
173 | When things get warm, they expand and become less dense, and when things
186 | cool, they condense and become denser. When an air mass becomes warmer
198 | and less dense, it rises. Alternatively, when an air mass becomes cooler and
211 | denser, it falls. (#3)

B

214 | **The Movement of Air Masses as a Factor in the Weather**
225 | Air masses are constantly moving. This constant movement causes weather. As
236 | a warm air mass rises, it carries water vapor up into the atmosphere. Then, the
251 | water vapor in the air begins to cool and drops of water condense into bigger
266 | drops of water, eventually forming clouds. This process is called **condensation**.
277 | Once condensation has been completed, and the clouds have become heavier and
289 | heavier, the clouds produce precipitation (e.g., rain, snow, hail). (#4)
298 | When warm air masses and cold air masses collide with each other, they
311 | create a weather front and various kinds of weather happen. The nature of the
325 | weather depends upon where the air masses are located, which direction they
337 | are moving, and many other characteristics.

C

343 **Cold Weather Fronts**

346   A **cold weather front** occurs when a cold air mass moves quickly into a region
361   and pushes a warm air mass upward. When the colder, denser air rushes in to
376   take the place of the warmer, moisture-filled air, wind is produced, and tall,
390   puffy clouds are formed. Sometimes the characteristics (such as temperature
400   and density of water vapor) of the cold and warm air masses are greatly
414   different. As a result, stronger winds occur. The greater the differences, the
426   more violent the weather will be. Sometimes, the cold front factors even lead to
440   hurricanes or tornadoes. Usually, this bad weather doesn't last very long. (#5)

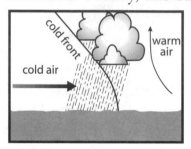 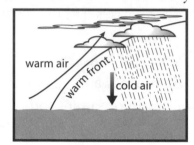

D

451 **Warm Weather Fronts**

454   A **warm weather front** occurs when a warm air mass moves quickly into a
468   region, bumps into a cold air mass, and rises up over the top of the cold air
485   mass. When the warm air rises high enough, clouds form and rain begins to fall.
500   The rain can last for many days. Typically, however, the warm front is associated
514   with less violent weather than that caused by a cold front. (#6)

E

525 **The Land as a Factor in the Weather**

533   An air mass above a particular piece of land becomes the same temperature
546   as that land. Dark-colored areas of the earth, including mountains, plowed
558   fields, and pavement, tend to absorb more of the sun's energy, so these surfaces
572   are warmer, and the air masses above these surfaces are warmer. Glaciers,
584   snowfields, and even plants tend to reflect the sun's energy back into space, so
598   these surfaces are cooler, and the air masses above them are cooler. Because
611   cities and farmlands are dark-colored areas, they tend to heat up and create
625   drying winds. These winds dry the land further. This phenomenon might even
637   harm the farmland's productivity. Careful planning can make a big difference in
649   the kind of weather the land creates. (#7)

F

656 **The Sun and the Seasons as Factors in the Weather**

666   Although the sun affects the temperature of the land and the accompanying
678   air masses, seasons cause changes in weather patterns, too. During different

689 | times of the year and on different parts of the planet, the earth receives more or
705 | less sunlight. This change in sunlight leads to differences in temperature, but
717 | also affects how much water evaporates into the air, as well as the nature and
732 | direction of the winds. (#8)

G

736 | **The Jet Stream as a Factor in the Weather**
745 | Finally, the weather is affected by changes in the jet stream. The **jet stream**
759 | is a fast-flowing river of air that circles the planet from west to east at speeds of
777 | 100 to 200 miles per hour. The speed and location of the jet stream is changed
793 | by the interaction of cold air masses to its north and warmer air masses to its
809 | south. Some of these changes are so extreme that the weather can be very
823 | different from year to year. (#9)

H

828 | **Predicting the Weather**
831 | The weather as it occurs across years is known as the climate. Different areas
845 | will be warmer or cooler, wetter or drier. These areas will then create different
859 | weather and climatic conditions. Climatologists study these conditions over
868 | many, many years. Clues to past climatic patterns are found in the chemistry of
882 | ice as well as in fossils. With the aid of supercomputers, climatologists are
895 | continuously creating a complex model of how the climate behaves. While the
907 | current model is far from completion, climatologists use the model to predict
919 | the weather. (#10)
921

(**ACTIVITY D**) *Fluency Building*

| Cold Timing | | Practice 1 | |
| Practice 2 | | Hot Timing | |

13

ACTIVITY E *Comprehension Questions—Multiple Choice*

Comprehension Strategy—Multiple Choice

Step 1: Read the item.

Step 2: Read all of the choices.

Step 3: Think about why each choice might be correct or incorrect. Check the article as needed.

Step 4: From the possible correct choices, select the best answer.

1. (Vocabulary) **The word "meteorologist" has two meaningful parts: "meteor" and "ologist." These parts mean:**

   a. atmosphere + people who study

   b. meteorites + people who study

   c. people who study + measurement

   d. meteor + scientists

2. (Cause and effect) **Which of these relationships is <u>NOT</u> true?**

   a. Dark-colored areas of the earth absorb more of the sun's energy and, as a result, these surfaces are warmer.

   b. When a warm front occurs, violent weather conditions such as hurricanes occur.

   c. When condensation is completed, clouds become heavier, and precipitation is produced.

   d. Changes in sunlight lead to changes in temperatures.

3. (Compare and contrast) **Which diagram best represents a cold front?**

   a.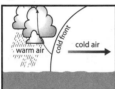

   b.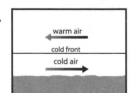

   c.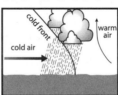

   d.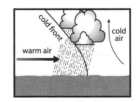

4. (Main Idea) **The main idea of this article is best stated as:**

   a. The sun affects temperature, evaporation, and the direction of winds.

   b. Weather is affected by many factors, including the movement of air masses, the land, the energy of the sun, seasons, and the jet stream.

   c. To understand changes in weather you only need to understand cold and warm weather fronts.

   d. Climatologists have studied different weather patterns for many years.

MULTIPLE CHOICE COMPREHENSION   **4**

(**ACTIVITY F**) *Vocabulary*

Yes/No/Why

1. Does **condensation accompany precipitation?**

_____

_____

_____

_____

2. Would **meteorologists frequently** study viruses?

_____

_____

_____

_____

3. Would the work of **meteorologists** and **climatologists** be **associated?**

_____

_____

_____

_____

Completion Activities

1. **direct:** to manage or control the course
   Some of the things that a person could direct include

   _____

   _____

   _____

   _____

2. **predict:** to declare beforehand
   If you were going to predict the winner of a football game, you might want to know

   _____

   _____

   _____

   _____

3. **productivity:** the ability to produce a lot
   The productivity of a factory could be improved by

   _____

   _____

   _____

   _____

4. **completion:** the end; the state of being finished
   Projects that you have seen through to completion include

   _____

   _____

   _____

   _____

VOCABULARY | **7**

(ACTIVITY G) *Expository Writing—Multi-Paragraph Answer*

Writing Strategy—Multi-Paragraph Answer

Step 1: LIST (List the details that are important enough to include in your answer.)

Step 2: CROSS OUT (Reread the details. Cross out any that don't go with the topic.)

Step 3: CONNECT (Connect any details that could go into one sentence.)

Step 4: NUMBER (Number the details in a logical order.)

Step 5: WRITE (Write the paragraph.)

Step 6: EDIT (Revise and proofread your answer.)

Prompt: Describe how the movement of air masses, the land, and the sun affect weather on the earth.

Plan: Complete the Planning Box.

Example Multi-Paragraph Plan

Planning Box
(topic a)
(detail)
(detail)
(detail)
(detail)
(detail)
(detail)
(detail)
(topic b)
(detail)
(detail)
(detail)
(detail)
(detail)
(detail)
(topic c)
(detail)
(detail)
(detail)
(detail)

Write: Write paragraphs a, b, and c on a separate piece of paper.

Evaluate: Evaluate the paragraphs using this rubric.

Rubric— Multi-Paragraph Answer	Student or Partner Rating	Teacher Rating
1. Did the author state the topic in the first sentence?	a. Yes Fix up b. Yes Fix up c. Yes Fix up	a. Yes No b. Yes No c. Yes No
2. Did the author include details that go with the topic?	a. Yes Fix up b. Yes Fix up c. Yes Fix up	a. Yes No b. Yes No c. Yes No
3. Did the author combine details in some of the sentences?	a. Yes Fix up b. Yes Fix up c. Yes Fix up	a. Yes No b. Yes No c. Yes No
4. Is the answer easy to understand?	Yes Fix up	Yes No
5. Did the author correctly spell words, particularly the words found in the article?	Yes Fix up	Yes No
6. Did the author use correct capitalization, capitalizing the first word in the sentence and proper names of people, places, and things?	Yes Fix up	Yes No
7. Did the author use correct punctuation, including a period at the end of each sentence?	Yes Fix up	Yes No

(ACTIVITY H) *Comprehension—Single-Paragraph Answer*

Writing Strategy—Single-Paragraph Answer

Step 1: Read the item.
Step 2: Turn the question into part of the answer and write it down.
Step 3: Think of the answer or locate the answer in the article.
Step 4: Complete your answer.

Prompt:

What Is—The land affects weather.

What If—What would happen to the weather if more and more cities were built in a particular area?

Write and Discuss: Write a paragraph. Then share your ideas. Use the Discussion Guidelines.

Discussion Guidelines

Speaker		Listener	
Looks like:	**Sounds like:**	**Looks like:**	**Sounds like:**
• Facing peers • Making eye contact • Participating	• Using pleasant, easy-to-hear voice • Sharing opinions, supporting facts and reasons from the article and from your experience • Staying on the topic	• Facing speaker • Making eye contact • Participating	• Waiting quietly to speak • Giving positive, supportive comments • Disagreeing respectfully

WRITING   DISCUSSION

4   4

Points   *Points*

(ACTIVITY A) *Vocabulary*

List 1: Tell

1.	canopy	*n.* ▶	(a covering)
2.	emergent	*adj.* ▶	(rising or coming out of)
3.	understory	*n.* ▶	(smaller trees that grow beneath big trees in the forest)

List 2: Strategy Practice

1.	precious	*adj.* ▶	(having great value)
2.	abundant	*adj.* ▶	(plentiful)
3.	diversity	*n.* ▶	(variety)
4.	comfortable	*adj.* ▶	(free from worry; at ease)
5.	consequently	*adv.* ▶	(as a result)
6.	portion	*n.* ▶	(part of a whole)
7.	deforestation	*n.* ▶	(the clearing of forests)
8.	undesirable	*adj.* ▶	(unwanted)
9.	maturity	*n.* ▶	(full growth and development)
10.	penetrating	*v.* ▶	(passing through)

List 3: Word Relatives

	Verb	Noun	Adjective
Family 1	prefer (to like better)	preference	preferable
Family 2	decompose (to rot)	decomposition decomposer	decomposable
Family 3	destroy (to ruin completely; to cause to go away; to end)	destruction	destructive destructible
Family 4	contribute (to give)	contribution contributor	contributable
Family 5	inhabit (to live in a place)	inhabitant	inhabitable

ACTIVITY B *Spelling Dictation*

1.	4.
2.	5.
3.	6.

SPELLING   6

Points

ACTIVITY C *Passage Reading and Comprehension*

Note: For this activity, you will need Reproducible N found in the *Teacher's Guide*.

Tropical Rainforests

A

11
25
37
50

Tropical rainforests are ecosystems located near the equator. They cover about 7% of the earth's total land area. These rainforests grow near the equator in more than 85 countries in Africa, Southeast Asia, and Central and South America. Even though they cover a relatively small portion of the earth, tropical rainforests contain between 50% and 90% of the world's species. (#1)

B

60
62
73
85

Rainforest Layers

Tropical rainforests are divided into four layers. Each layer has specific characteristics that provide unique food and shelter not found in the other layers. Therefore, each layer has its own diverse and unique group of species.

emergent

canopy

understory

forest floor

98
112
126

The **emergent layer** is the topmost layer. Here is where the tops of the tallest trees emerge from the canopy below. These trees are some of the tallest in the forest, often reaching a height of 200 feet or more. Many of them have

142	broad green leaves, which catch a great deal of sunlight. Animals also live at this
157	highest layer of the forest. Butterflies, eagles, and bats are comfortable flying at
170	these heights. Some types of monkeys prefer the tops of the trees. Other tree-
184	dwellers, such as lizards and flying squirrels, may also be found at the emergent
198	layer. (#2)
C 199	Traveling downwards from the emergent layer, we find the **canopy layer**.
210	The canopy is a dense cluster of trees with smooth oval leaves. These trees block
225	most of the sunlight and keep it from penetrating to lower levels. The trees in
240	the canopy layer are not as tall as the trees of the emergent layer. Trees in the
257	canopy layer reach maturity at 75 to 90 feet. Food is abundant in these smaller,
272	mature trees. Monkeys, snakes, treefrogs, and birds populate this layer. (#3)
D 282	Below the canopy layer is the **understory**. Very little sunlight reaches the
294	plants found in the understory layer because of the dense canopy layer above.
307	Unlike the higher layers, which are drier, hot, and very windy, the understory layer
321	is humid (moist) and quite still. Moisture collects at these lower levels and does
335	not evaporate easily. The trees in this layer do not grow very tall at all, seldom
351	reaching 12 feet. They often have broad, flat leaves that catch as much light as
366	possible in this shadowy layer. Even though little light shines into the understory, a
380	lot of life exists there. Many animals feed on fruits and leaves from shrubs or small
396	trees. Some animals, such as leopards and jaguars, feed on smaller animals. Many
409	types of insects favor this layer of the tropical rainforest. (#4)
E 419	At the bottom of the tropical rainforest, we find the **forest floor**. Here, the
433	ground is made up of decaying matter from the upper layers. The sunlight
446	cannot shine easily through the three layers above, so it is very dark at this
461	lowest layer. Few green plants can thrive here. Consequently, the forest floor
473	has poor soil. Many insects live on the floor, feeding on the dead and
487	decomposing wood, leaves, and other matter. Some larger animals, such as the
499	giant anteater, feed on the insects that live in this layer. (#5)
F	
510	**Concern for the Rainforests**
514	People have good reason to be concerned about destruction of the
525	rainforests. Many of the world's tropical rainforests are rapidly disappearing.
535	Rainforests are being chopped down for wood and farmland. Scientists have said
547	that deforestation, or removal of the forests' trees, may have a greater impact on
561	the rest of the world than anyone realizes. All organisms that make up the
575	rainforest ecosystem affect and create the weather and climate of that region.
587	The climate created by a rainforest also affects the weather and climate in other
601	parts of the world. (#6)

605	Many scientists believe that tropical rainforests are essential for preventing
615	serious global warming. Trees take in carbon dioxide (a harmful gas which
627	contributes to global warming) and release oxygen into the atmosphere. Their
638	leaves reflect heat energy back into space. As the rainforests are destroyed,
650	fewer trees are available to take in carbon dioxide and to release oxygen, and
664	more heat is present in our atmosphere. The destruction of rainforests will upset
677	weather patterns and alter the amounts of certain gasses in the air, thus
690	increasing the rate of global warming. As a result, the overall temperatures on
703	the earth may rise and produce undesirable changes in the earth's weather
715	patterns. The graph below shows how much warmer or colder than normal it
728	has been when measurements from thousands of meteorological stations are
738	combined. (#7)

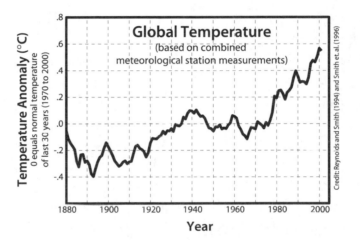

739	In addition, many scientists feel that the rich diversity of plant life in the
753	tropical rainforests may hold the key to major medical breakthroughs.
763	Nevertheless, these plants are being destroyed before we have the chance to
775	understand their potential. Tropical rainforests and their inhabitants are
784	disappearing at an alarming rate. It is important to conserve these precious and
797	vital resources. (#8)
799	

(ACTIVITY D) *Fluency Building*

Cold Timing [   ]   **Practice 1** [   ]

Practice 2 [   ]   **Hot Timing** [   ]

(ACTIVITY E) *Comprehension Questions—Multiple Choice*

Comprehension Strategy—Multiple Choice

Step 1: Read the item.

Step 2: Read all of the choices.

Step 3: Think about why each choice might be correct or incorrect. Check the article as needed.

Step 4: From the possible correct choices, select the best answer.

1. (Vocabulary) **Which set of words would best represent tropical rain forests?**

   a. canopy layer   **c.** emergent layer
   emergent layer   canopy layer
   understory   forest floor
   forest floor   understory

   b. forest floor   **d.** tallest trees
   understory   humid layer
   canopy layer   cluster of trees
   emergent layer   decaying matter

2. (Cause and effect) **Many scientists are concerned about deforestation of rainforests because:**

   a. rainforests could be used for farmlands if preserved.

   b. rainforests are one of the few pristine vacation spots available.

   c. rainforests have a rich diversity of plants and animals that will be lost.

   d. rainforests currently cover 50 to 90% of the land.

3. (Cause and effect) **Which of these relationships is <u>false</u>?**

   a. Because the emergent layer has the tallest trees, it is inhabited with eagles, bats, and monkeys.

   b. Because the canopy layer has mature trees, food is abundant.

   c. Because the understory has little sunlight, moisture collects, and it is very humid.

   d. Because sunlight cannot penetrate the forest floor, green plants thrive.

4. (Main Idea) **Tropical rainforests might hold the "key to major medical breakthroughs" because:**

   a. medicines are often developed from plants.

   b. cures might come from the animals that feed on the plants.

   c. the study of the plants' cells could let us know about the cells of humans.

   d. plants in rainforests may contain viruses.

MULTIPLE CHOICE COMPREHENSION

(ACTIVITY F) *Vocabulary Activities*

Yes/No/Why

1. Are there **abundant** trees in the **understory?**

_____

_____

_____

_____

2. Is **deforestation undesirable?**

_____

_____

_____

_____

3. Is it possible that **emergent** values could result from reaching **maturity?**

_____

_____

_____

_____

Completion Activities

1. **precious:** having great value
Some of the things that a person considers to be precious may include

_____

_____

_____

_____

2. **contribute:** to give
The best way that you could contribute to the world would be to

_____

_____

_____

_____

3. **penetrating:** passing through
Penetrating light could pass through

_____

_____

_____

_____

4. **comfortable:** free from worry; at ease
In a new situation, I would feel more comfortable if

_____

_____

_____

_____

VOCABULARY 7

Points

(ACTIVITY G) *Expository Writing—Multi-Paragraph Answer*

Writing Strategy—Multi-Paragraph Answer

Step 1: LIST (List the details that are important enough to include in your answer.)

Step 2: CROSS OUT (Reread the details. Cross out any that don't go with the topic.)

Step 3: CONNECT (Connect any details that could go into one sentence.)

Step 4: NUMBER (Number the details in a logical order.)

Step 5: WRITE (Write the paragraph.)

Step 6: EDIT (Revise and proofread your answer.)

Prompt: Write one paragraph summarizing information about the four layers of the rainforest and one paragraph about scientists' concerns about the destruction of the rainforests.

Plan: Complete the Planning Box.

Example Multi-Paragraph Plan

Planning Box
(topic a)
(detail)
(detail)
(detail)
(detail)
(detail)
(detail)
(detail)
(detail)
(detail)
(detail)
(detail)
(detail)
(topic b)
(detail)
(detail)
(detail)
(detail)
(detail)
(detail)

Write: Write paragraphs a and b on a separate piece of paper.

Evaluate: Evaluate the paragraphs using this rubric.

Rubric— Multi-Paragraph Answer	Student or Partner Rating	Teacher Rating
1. Did the author state the topic in the first sentence?	a. Yes Fix up b. Yes Fix up c. Yes Fix up	a. Yes No b. Yes No c. Yes No
2. Did the author include details that go with the topic?	a. Yes Fix up b. Yes Fix up c. Yes Fix up	a. Yes No b. Yes No c. Yes No
3. Did the author combine details in some of the sentences?	a. Yes Fix up b. Yes Fix up c. Yes Fix up	a. Yes No b. Yes No c. Yes No
4. Is the answer easy to understand?	Yes Fix up	Yes No
5. Did the author correctly spell words, particularly the words found in the article?	Yes Fix up	Yes No
6. Did the author use correct capitalization, capitalizing the first word in the sentence and proper names of people, places, and things?	Yes Fix up	Yes No
7. Did the author use correct punctuation, including a period at the end of each sentence?	Yes Fix up	Yes No

WRITING   13
Points

ACTIVITY H *Comprehension—Single-Paragraph Answer*

Writing Strategy—Single-Paragraph Answer

Step 1: Read the item.
Step 2: Turn the question into part of the answer and write it down.
Step 3: Think of the answer or locate the answer in the article.
Step 4: Complete your answer.

Prompt:

What Is—Rainforests are being cut down at an alarming rate.

What If—What would happen if most of the earth's rainforests were cut down? (Hint: Think about ecosystems, energy and matter, and weather.)

Write and Discuss: Write a paragraph. Then share your ideas. Use the Discussion Guidelines.

Discussion Guidelines

Speaker		Listener	
Looks like:	**Sounds like:**	**Looks like:**	**Sounds like:**
• Facing peers • Making eye contact • Participating	• Using pleasant, easy-to-hear voice • Sharing opinions, supporting facts and reasons from the article and from your experience • Staying on the topic	• Facing speaker • Making eye contact • Participating	• Waiting quietly to speak • Giving positive, supportive comments • Disagreeing respectfully

WRITING   DISCUSSION

4	4
Points	Points

ACTIVITY A Vocabulary

List 1: Tell

1. **industrialized**   *adj.* ▶ (related to business)
2. **Exxon Valdez**   *n.* ▶ (an oil tanker that ran aground in Prince William Sound)
3. **consequences**   *n.* ▶ (results of earlier actions)
4. **mechanical**   *adj.* ▶ (having to do with machinery)
5. **rescuers**   *n.* ▶ (people who save other beings)
6. **aquatic**   *adj.* ▶ (related to water)
7. **buoyancy**   *n.* ▶ (the ability to float or rise in water)
8. **aquarium**   *n.* ▶ (a place that houses fish, water animals, and water plants)

List 2: Strategy Practice

1. **containment**   *n.* ▶ (to keep from spreading)
2. **deliberate**   *adj.* ▶ (carefully planned)
3. **encountered**   *v.* ▶ (met unexpectedly)
4. **similarly**   *adv.* ▶ (being alike)
5. **fossilization**   *n.* ▶ (the act of becoming a fossil)
6. **minimize**   *v.* ▶ (to lessen)
7. **monitored**   *v.* ▶ (watched)
8. **pollution**   *n.* ▶ (something that makes something else dirty or impure)
9. **replenish**   *v.* ▶ (to provide a new supply)
10. **unfortunately**   *adv.* ▶ (unluckily)

TALLY ☐   VOCABULARY 5

Points   *Student Book: Application Lesson 15* **183**

List 3: Word Relatives

	Verb	Noun	Adjective
Family 1	include (to put in a group)	inclusion	inclusive
Family 2	sabotage (to damage or destroy deliberately)	sabotage saboteur	
Family 3	locate (to discover the exact place of)	location locater	
Family 4	dispose (to get rid of or throw away)	disposal	disposable
Family 5	attend (to fix one's thoughts on something)	attention	attentive

(ACTIVITY B) Spelling Dictation

1.	4.
2.	5.
3.	6.

SPELLING   **6**
Points

ACTIVITY C *Passage Reading and Comprehension*

Note: For this activity, you will need Reproducible O found in the *Teacher's Guide*.

Oil Spills

A

16   Oil is a resource that is used by most people in the world to some extent.
26 The United States, Canada, Australia, Great Britain, Germany, and other
38 industrialized countries, however, use great quantities of oil. Because oil is the
53 end result of a long natural process called **fossilization**, it takes many years for oil
68 to be formed. Oil is found only in certain areas of the world, including the
83 bottoms of oceans. It can be very expensive to remove the oil from the ground
    and from under the ocean floor. (#1)

B

89 **Causes of Oil Spills**
93   Once oil is removed, it must be transported to the country where it is going
108 to be used. Huge ships, called **oil tankers**, transport oil over the world's
121 waterways. Unfortunately, accidents occur, and oil is spilled into the seas and
133 waterways. In March of 1989, the Exxon Valdez oil tanker ran aground in Prince
147 William Sound, Alaska. Almost 11 million gallons of oil spilled out of the tanker
161 and into the water. That's enough oil to fill up 430 classrooms! Although that was
176 the largest tanker spill in the waters of the United States, nearly 14,000 oil spills
191 occur worldwide each year. (#2)
195   Sometimes the spills are caused by mistakes on the part of people. For
208 example, the Exxon Valdez ran aground because the man steering the boat did
221 not follow an order to change his course. Sometimes spills are a result of bad
236 equipment or old ships. Poor weather conditions can cause a ship to run
249 aground and spill oil. Oil spills can also be the result of deliberate sabotage or
264 illegal dumping. (#3)

C

266 **Consequences of Oil Spills**
270   The spilled oil spreads out across the surface of the water, where it floats in a
286 thin layer called an **oil slick**. As it spreads more and more thinly, it resembles a
302 rainbow on the surface of the water. This rainbow is called a **sheen**.
315   Oil spills can be extremely dangerous for marine animals. Marine mammals
326 and birds depend on their fur and feathers to keep them warm and dry. When
341 their fur or feathers become oiled, they lose the ability to repel water. The
355 animals can no longer keep warm or float as easily. Animals and birds may also
370 ingest (swallow) the oil when they try to clean themselves. The oil can poison

384	them. Similarly, fish and bottom-dwellers may experience the oil as toxic and
397	may develop long-term diseases or reproductive problems. An even more
408	serious consequence results when oil kills the plankton. **Plankton** are tiny
419	organisms that produce much of our oxygen and serve as the base of aquatic
433	food webs. (#4)

D

435	**Response to Oil Spills**
439	The first step in reducing the impact of an oil spill is to contain the spill at its
457	source. Containment helps to limit the amount of damage the spill causes.
469	Local, state, and federal agencies as well as volunteers move into the area
482	immediately. The next step is to begin wildlife rescue and clean-up efforts. (#5)
495	Rescuers begin by trying to keep unharmed wildlife away from contaminated
506	areas. They use devices designed to scare wildlife away from a given area. Then
520	rescuers turn their attention to the wildlife that has already encountered the oil.
533	Birds and marine mammals are captured by wildlife experts and taken to nearby
546	treatment centers. At these centers, officials and volunteers do their best to
558	flush oil from the animals' eyes and intestines and to minimize the stress such a
573	crisis can cause. Special procedures are used for gradually washing the oil out of
587	animals' feathers or fur and allowing their bodies to replenish the natural oils
600	necessary to provide warmth and buoyancy. (#6)
606	The animals' health and nutrition are carefully monitored to help the natural
618	healing process. After they have regained their health and their body coverings
630	have returned to normal, the animals may be tagged for tracking, and then
643	released into an appropriate habitat. Sometimes, if animals are very sick, or too
656	young to be released on their own, they may be given to an aquarium or a
672	wildlife center for care. (#7)

E

676 **Cleaning the Spill**
679   Depending on the location and conditions of the spill, several techniques can
691 be used to clean it up. Mechanical containment techniques include equipment
702 designed to capture the spilled oil so that it can be disposed of properly.
716 Chemical and biological methods are used to change the composition of the oil
729 and help it break down faster. Physical methods are used to clean up shorelines.
743 These methods include wiping, washing, scrubbing, and raking the oil. (#8)

F

753 **Prevention**
754   Federal regulations are designed to help prevent large-scale spills like that of
767 the Exxon Valdez. Most oil pollution of water, however, comes from the
779 mishandling of oil products. Although 37 million gallons of oil are spilled into
792 the ocean each year, regular people pour over 360 million gallons of oil down
806 drains that lead to waterways. Proper disposal and recycling of used oils can go a
821 long way toward helping to prevent oil pollution in the water. (#9)
832

(ACTIVITY D) *Fluency Building*

Cold Timing		**Practice 1**	
Practice 2		**Hot Timing**	

ACTIVITY E *Comprehension Questions—Multiple Choice*

Comprehension Strategy—Multiple Choice

Step 1: Read the item.
Step 2: Read all of the choices.
Step 3: Think about why each choice might be correct or incorrect. Check the article as needed.
Step 4: From the possible correct choices, select the best answer.

1. (Cause and effect) **Which of these relationships is NOT accurate?**
   a. oil spill → oil on birds' feathers thus birds can't repel water thus can't keep warm.
   b. oil spill → oil on birds' feathers thus birds swallow oil when cleaning thus oil poisons them.
   c. oil spill → oil kills plankton thus food for ocean fish limited.
   d. oil spill → air is filled with oil thus birds can't breath air thus birds die of fumes.

2. (Cause and effect) **Oil spills are NOT caused by:**
   a. weather conditions that cause a ship to run aground.
   b. oil seeping out of the floor of the ocean.
   c. human mistakes on oil carriers.
   d. illegal dumping of oil from a ship.

3. (Main idea) **Which of these titles would best indicate the content covered in this article?**
   a. Oil Spills: Value and Danger
   b. Oil Spills: Whose Fault Is It?
   c. Oil Spills: Causes, Results, Solutions
   d. Oil Spills: Consequences to the Environment

4. (Cause and effect) **Which one of these would probably be the best plan for reducing the damage done by oil?**
   a. Try to reduce oil spills by <u>improving</u> the ships that carry oil, the weather information available to ships, and the quality of their crew.
   b. Improve the procedures for containing an oil spill at its source.
   c. Train rescuers to use a variety of devices to keep wildlife out of the contaminated area.
   d. Try to get people to stop pouring oil down drains that lead to waterways.

MULTIPLE CHOICE COMPREHENSION

4

Points

(ACTIVITY F) *Vocabulary*

Yes/No/Why

1. Would **containment** of **industrialized** nations **minimize** resource usage?

2. Would **deliberate monitoring** of the **Exxon Valdez** have reduced the **consequences**?

3. Does **pollution replenish aquariums?**

Completion Activities

1. sabotage: to damage or destroy deliberately
Some ways that you could sabotage getting a good grade in a class would include

_____

_____

_____

_____

2. locate: to discover the exact place of
When trying to locate a specific fact, you might

_____

_____

_____

_____

3. dispose: to get rid of or throw away
Some things that you should <u>never</u> dispose of include

_____

_____

_____

_____

4. monitored: watched
One thing that would need to be carefully monitored is

_____

_____

_____

_____

VOCABULARY 7
Points

(ACTIVITY G) *Expository Writing—Multi-Paragraph Answer*

Writing Strategy—Multi-Paragraph Answer

Step 1: LIST (List the details that are important enough to include in your answer.)

Step 2: CROSS OUT (Reread the details. Cross out any that don't go with the topic.)

Step 3: CONNECT (Connect any details that could go into one sentence.)

Step 4: NUMBER (Number the details in a logical order.)

Step 5: WRITE (Write the paragraph.)

Step 6: EDIT (Revise and proofread your answer.)

Prompt: Describe the causes, consequences, and responses to oil spills.

Plan: Complete the Planning Box.

Example Multi-Paragraph Plan

Planning Box
(topic a)
(detail)
(detail)
(detail)
(detail)
(detail)
(detail)
(topic b)
(detail)
(detail)
(detail)
(detail)
(detail)
(detail)
(topic c)
(detail)
(detail)
(detail)
(detail)
(detail)
(detail)

Write: Write paragraphs a, b, and c on a separate piece of paper.

Evaluate: Evaluate the paragraphs using this rubric.

Rubric— Multi-Paragraph Answer	Student or Partner Rating		Teacher Rating	
1. Did the author state the topic in the first sentence?	a. Yes Fix up b. Yes Fix up c. Yes Fix up		a. Yes No b. Yes No c. Yes No	
2. Did the author include details that go with the topic?	a. Yes Fix up b. Yes Fix up c. Yes Fix up		a. Yes No b. Yes No c. Yes No	
3. Did the author combine details in some of the sentences?	a. Yes Fix up b. Yes Fix up c. Yes Fix up		a. Yes No b. Yes No c. Yes No	
4. Is the answer easy to understand?	Yes Fix up		Yes No	
5. Did the author correctly spell words, particularly the words found in the article?	Yes Fix up		Yes No	
6. Did the author use correct capitalization, capitalizing the first word in the sentence and proper names of people, places, and things?	Yes Fix up		Yes No	
7. Did the author use correct punctuation, including a period at the end of each sentence?	Yes Fix up		Yes No	

WRITING 13
Points

ACTIVITY H *Comprehension—Single-Paragraph Answer*

Writing Strategy—Single-Paragraph Answer

Step 1: Read the item.
Step 2: Turn the question into part of the answer and write it down.
Step 3: Think of the answer or locate the answer in the article.
Step 4: Complete your answer.

Prompt:

What Is—In the movement of oil from one country to another, oil spills are a fairly frequent occurrence.

What if—What if you were asked to outline a plan to prevent future oil spills from happening? What would you suggest?

Write and Discuss: Write a paragraph. Then share your ideas. Use the Discussion Guidelines.

Discussion Guidelines

Speaker		Listener	
Looks like:	**Sounds like:**	**Looks like:**	**Sounds like:**
• Facing peers • Making eye contact • Participating	• Using pleasant, easy-to-hear voice • Sharing opinions, supporting facts and reasons from the article and from your experience • Staying on the topic	• Facing speaker • Making eye contact • Participating	• Waiting quietly to speak • Giving positive, supportive comments • Disagreeing respectfully

WRITING   DISCUSSION

4	4
Points	*Points*

REWARDS Strategies for Reading Long Words

Overt Strategy

1. Circle the word parts (prefixes) at the beginning of the word.

2. Circle the word parts (suffixes) at the end of the word.

3. Underline the letters for vowel sounds in the rest of the word.

4. Say the parts of the word.

5. Say the parts fast.

6. Make it a real word.

Example:

(re)(con)struc(tion)

Covert Strategy

1. Look for word parts at the beginning and end of the word and vowel sounds in the rest of the word.

2. Say the parts of the word.

3. Say the parts fast.

4. Make it a real word.

Word Parts and Vowel Combinations Reference Chart

	Word Part	Key Word	Word Part	Key Word	Word Part	Key Word
Word Parts at the Beginning of Words	a	above	com	compare	mis	mistaken
	ab	abdomen	con	continue	multi	multiage
	ac	accommodate	de	depart	over	overpopulate
	ad	advertise	dis	discover	per	permit
	af	afford	en	entail	pre	prevent
	ap	appreciate	ex	example	pro	protect
	ar	arrange	hydro	hydrothermal	re	return
	as	associate	im	immediate	sub	submarine
	at	attention	in	insert	trans	translate
	auto	automatic	ir	irregular	un	uncover
	be	belong	micro	microscope		
Word Parts at the End of Words	able	disposable	ful	careful	ness	kindness
	age	courage	ible	reversible	or	tailor
	al	final	ic	frantic	ous	nervous
	ance	disturbance	ing	running	s	birds
	ant	dormant	ion	million	ship	ownership
	ate	regulate	ish	selfish	sion	mission
	ary	military	ism	realism	sive	expensive
	cial	special	ist	artist	tial	partial
	cious	precious	ity	oddity	tive	attentive
	ed	landed	ize	criticize	tion	action
	ence	essence	le	cradle	tious	cautious
	ent	consistent	less	useless	ture	picture
	er	farmer	ly	safely	y	industry
	est	biggest	ment	argument		
Vowel Combinations	ai	rain	ou	loud	a–e	make
	au	sauce	ow	low, down	e–e	Pete
	ay	say	oy	boy	i–e	side
	ee	deep	ar	farm	o–e	hope
	ea	meat, thread	er	her	u–e	use
	oa	foam	ir	bird		
	oi	void	or	torn		
	oo	moon, book	ur	turn		

Review Lessons Chart

Name _____   Teacher _____

	Activities A–C _____ (4 possible Participation Points)	Activities D and E _____ (4 possible Participation Points)	Activity F Reading Check _____ (4 possible Performance Points)	SUBTOTAL POINTS _____ (12 possible points)	BONUS POINTS	TOTAL POINTS	LESSON GRADE
Review Lesson 1							
Review Lesson 2							
Review Lesson 3							
Review Lesson 4							
Review Lesson 5							
Review Lesson 6							

Participation Points
(Possible Points: 4)

- Following behavioral guidelines
- Paying attention
- Participating
- Responding accurately

Performance Points
(Possible Points: 4)

No errors	**4 points**
1 error	**3 points**
2 errors	**2 points**
More than 2 errors	**0 points**

Application Lessons Chart

Name _____

Teacher _____

	Activity A List 1 and List 2 (4 possible Participation Points)	Oral Vocabulary Tally (5 possible Performance Points)	Activity A List 3 (4 possible Participation Points)	Activity B Spelling (6 possible Performance Points)	Activity D Passage Reading (4 possible Participation Points)	Activity E Fluency (4 possible Performance Points)	Activity F Multiple Choice (4 possible Performance Points)	Activity F Short Answer (4 possible Performance Points)	Activity G Writing (7 possible Performance Points)	SUBTOTAL POINTS (42 possible points)	BONUS POINTS	TOTAL POINTS	LESSON GRADE
Application Lesson 1								4					
Application Lesson 2								4					
Application Lesson 3								4					
Application Lesson 4													
Application Lesson 5													
Application Lesson 6													
Application Lesson 7													
Application Lesson 8													
Application Lesson 9													
Application Lesson 10													
Application Lesson 11													
Application Lesson 12													
Application Lesson 13													
Application Lesson 14													
Application Lesson 15													

Fluency Graph

Student Name: _____

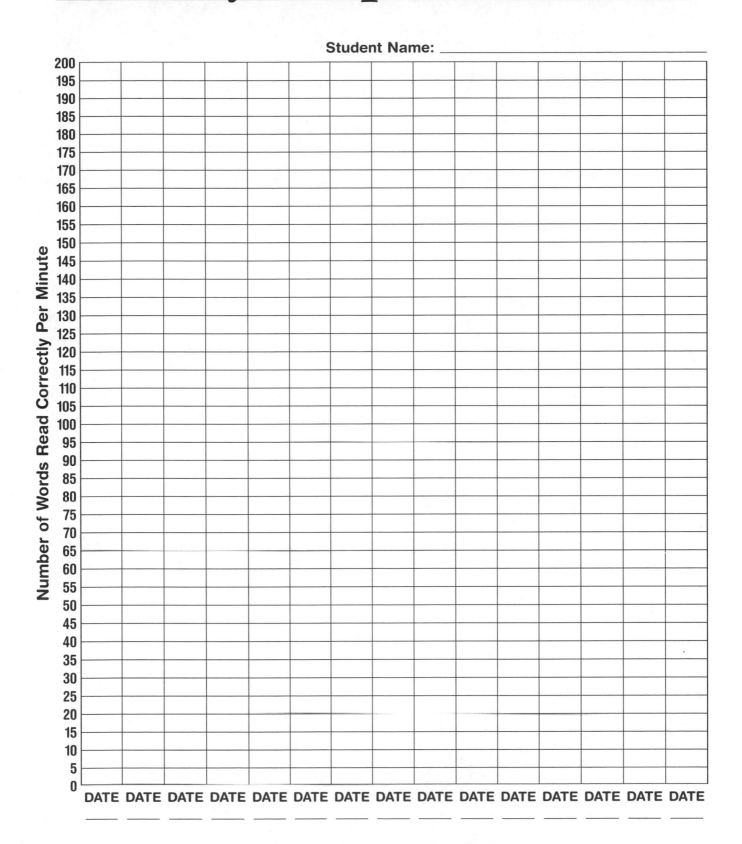

Number of Words Read Correctly Per Minute

200
195
190
185
180
175
170
165
160
155
150
145
140
135
130
125
120
115
110
105
100
95
90
85
80
75
70
65
60
55
50
45
40
35
30
25
20
15
10
5
0

DATE DATE DATE DATE DATE DATE DATE DATE DATE DATE DATE DATE DATE DATE DATE